Susan Campbell / Caroline Conran

Macmillan

First published 1971 by
MACMILLAN AND CO LIMITED
London and Basingstoke

First published 1982 by
PAPERMAC
a division of Macmillan Publishers Limited
London and Basingstoke

Associated companies in Auckland, Delhi, Dublin,
Gaborone, Hamburg, Harare, Hong Kong, Johannesburg,
Kuala Lumpur, Lagos, Manzini, Melbourne, Mexico City,
Nairobi, New York, Singapore and Tokyo

Reprinted 1983, 1985

ISBN 0 333 33176 1

Printed in Hong Kong

To Robin and Terence

Contents

Diagrams

Introduction

Everybody loves eating expensive food, but extravagant meals often mean crises in greedy households, and lead to eating cheap food which alas, needs far more care and attention to make it really good. Happily people who love cooking like the challenge of making the most of humble ingredients, and positively enjoy turning a plain packet of semolina into a dish of melting, fragrant gnocchi, and this is what the book is about.

Although there is obviously no stopping convenience foods, turning to the shelves of the supermarket does not save you anything but time, since the pre-packed foods have been expensively prepared by other people, however cheaply they may have been bought in their original state, and are lavishly packaged and advertised. And if the people who enjoy feeding their families continue to carry their shopping baskets stead-fastly past the supermarket door, in search of the odder cheap ingredients, then the shops will go on selling them, but if nobody asks for things like belly of pork and breast of lamb they will soon disappear for ever.

Eating cheaply does not mean buying inferior expensive ingredients, but good cheap ones. To cook them properly and keep the finished dish consistent with the idea of good eating, it is essential to have the right basic raw materials. This list of basics for a family store-cupboard includes necessities for the preparation of foods that need a helping hand to make them taste and look their best.

Acknowledgments

To butchers Sidney Norwood and Frederick Lovell for their help with the meat diagrams, and to Miss Emily Spencer for experienced help in the kitchen, to Carol Amos and Patricia Moran for all kinds of patient work, and to many friends who contributed recipes.

Basics

Cheap **butter** for cooking
A large tin of **olive oil** (cheaper by the gallon)
A large tin of **arachide oil** for deep frying. Keep
  separate bottles, one for fish and one for other
  things, and always strain the oil before it goes back
  in the bottle, or it will not stay fresh
Large chunk of **Parmesan cheese**
Tins and tins of Italian peeled **tomatoes**
Tubes or tins of **tomato purée**
Packets of **pasta** and **semolina**
Pounds of dried **haricot beans, kidney beans,**
  flageolets etc
Rice, long-grain for curry, Italian for risotto, round
  for puddings
Large bag of **dried mushrooms,** better than tinned
  and cheaper
Spices : coriander, cumin, turmeric, cardamom,
  chilli, paprika, allspice, mixed spice, cloves,
  cinnamon sticks, mace, nutmeg
Herbs (do not keep them too long) : bay leaves on
  a branch, rosemary, thyme, oregano, basil,
  marjoram, sage, tarragon. Keep parsley, chives
  and mint fresh in polythene bags in the refrigerator

Stock cubes chicken and beef. Maggi are best
Garlic
Tins of **tunny fish, anchovies** in oil, **sardines,**
  pimentoes
Dijon **mustard, mustard powder**
Sea salt, peppercorns
Olives : buy them loose and keep them fresh in a
  jar of oil
Plain flour and **baking powder,** so you do not
  have to worry about self-raising flour
Dried yeast or fresh yeast from the baker which
  keeps for up to a week in the refrigerator
Vanilla sugar : keep a pod of vanilla in a jar of
  caster sugar, and top it up as you need to
Wine vinegar
Dried fruit
Saffron, pine nuts, pistachio nuts, juniper
  berries and **truffles** are all cheaper bought
  abroad

(Don't keep anything for more than six months, or a
  year at most)

Meat Roasting Table

Meat	Quick Roast	Slow Roast	
	For good quality meat. Sear at Reg 8/450° for 15 minutes. Reduce to Reg 5/375° for the remainder of the cooking time.	Best for poor quality joints. It helps make them tender. Roast at Reg 3/325°.	N.B. Bone is a good conductor of heat, so meat with the bone in does not need the extra minutes over. Stuffing on the other hand is a poor conductor of heat, so joints that are stuffed need perhaps fifteen minutes extra, depending on the thickness of the stuffing. You should always judge by the shape of the joint that is to be cooked. If it is a long thin piece of meat it will obviously need less cooking than a compact thick piece. So use the chart as a general guide, supported by your own judgment.
Beef	15 minutes per lb plus 15 minutes for rare roasting. 20 minutes per lb plus 20 minutes for meat well done.	40 minutes per lb plus 45 minutes.	
Lamb	25 minutes per lb plus 25 minutes.	45 minutes per lb plus 45 minutes.	
Pork	35 minutes per lb plus 35 minutes.	Not suitable.	
Veal	30 minutes per lb plus 30 minutes.	50 minutes per lb plus 50 minutes.	
Chicken	20 minutes per lb plus 20 minutes.	Over 4 lb, 25 minutes per lb plus 25 minutes.	
Turkey	8-10 lb bird 2-2½ hours 10-14 lb bird 2½-3 hours 14-20 lb bird 3½-4 hours	8-10 lb bird 3-3½ hours 10-14 lb bird 3½-4 hours 14-20 lb bird 4½-5 hours	

The Metric System

Conversion tables for measurements and temperatures.

Weight

1 oz —	28·35 g	1 kilogramme — 1000 g —	2 lb 3 oz	approx
2 oz —	56·7 g	500 g —	1 lb 1½ oz	,,
¼ lb —	113·4 g	250 g —	9 oz	,,
½ lb —	226·8 g	125 g —	4½ oz	,,
12 oz —	340·2 g	100 g —	3½ oz	,,
16 oz —	453·6 g	25 g —	1 oz	,,

Liquids

¼ pt (1 gill) — 142 ml			
½ pt — 284 ml			
1 pt — 568 ml			
1 litre —	1000 g —	1¾ pt — 35 fl oz	approx
½ litre —	500 g —	¾ pt plus 4½ tablespoons	,,
¼ litre —	250 g —	½ pt less 2 tablespoons	,,
1 decilitre —	100 g —	6 tablespoons	,,
1 centilitre —	10 g —	1 dessertspoon	,,
1 millilitre —	1 g —	a few drops	,,
5 millilitres —	5 g —	pharmaceutical teaspoon	

Temperatures

Electricity and Solid Fuel	Gas	Degrees Fahrenheit	Degrees Centigrade
Cool	¼-½	250	121
Very slow	1	275	135
Slow	2	300	149
	3	325	163
Moderate	4	350	177
	5	375	190
Moderately hot	6	400	205
Hot	7	425	218
Very hot	8	450	232
	9	475	246

Soups

It is really easy to make home-made soup, and it's very odd how few people bother considering how much nicer it tastes than any out of a tin. The rustling of packets and clank of tin-openers may be a welcome sound from Tiger Bay to the Wash, but what appears in the soup-bowl a minute later has very little to do with the piping hot, delicately flavoured and beautifully coloured bowlful, with its handful of sizzling croûtons or swirl of cream, that is your own vegetable soup. And the money saved by the manufacturers in buying vegetables by the ton is spent on packaging and massive advertising, so ready-made soups are not particularly money-saving and should be kept for emergencies.

If you have a liquidiser, the making of soup is simply a question of cooking the right ingredients to the right degree of tenderness and then giving them a quick whizz, to purée them. If not, a Moulin-Légumes (or mouli), a small, inexpensive food mill for sieving soft fruit and cooked vegetables, is invaluable.

One of the vital ingredients for good soup is stock. Many cookery writers between the two wars decided stock should not be used in vegetable soups, because it overpowered the flavour of the vegetables and had a certain sameness to it that robbed the soup of its delicacy and freshness. It is certainly true that if you use a strongly-flavoured or not altogether fresh stock you will end up with an awful failure. So use your own simple, freshly-made stock, obtained by putting chicken carcasses and bones in cold water, with a few carrots and an onion, plus a sprig of parsley, peppercorns and a bay leaf, and letting the liquid simmer and reduce incredibly slowly while you just go away and leave it. You can do the same with meaty beef or veal bones, freshly bought from the butcher; try to get marrow bones if you can, and remember to ask him to chop them up for you. Strain the stock, keep it in the refrigerator and use it within a day or two, then make a fresh lot. Or if you have a deep-freeze, you can keep a reserve of concentrated stock always available. The day of the never-ending stock-pot to which a procession of old left-overs made its way daily is dead and gone; we don't like having that dreary, soggy-smelling dishwater in our kitchens any more, and anyway there isn't room for it. For vegetable soup chicken stock really is the best, and if you haven't any it is perfectly feasible to use a stock-cube (Maggi tastes less of monosodium glutamate than others) but dilute it much more than it says in the directions or you will find that good old packet-soup flavour lurking in your own lovingly-made soup. Chicken broth, as well as being the best stock, makes a marvellous basis for clear soups, and is a staple of many Italian kitchens, although one doesn't all that frequently get chicken to eat there. To it you can add pasta, poached eggs, marble-sized dumplings, finely sliced vegetables (which should be barely cooked when they are served), or a handful of rice and some egg-yolks beaten with fresh lemon juice. Do not, however, attempt a complicated mixture of different things or you may well end up with an indifferent sort of wet Russian salad.

The more filling soups, made with pasta and beans, meat and pearl barley, split peas and ham bones, should be served either as a meal on their own, with cheese and fruit afterwards, or before a very light, simple main dish such as an omelette or a salade Niçoise.

If you grow your own vegetables, you can use practically anything you have too much of to make a wonderful first course: French beans coming too fast to their best, lettuces that are getting ready to bolt, peas that have grown too fat, spinach you can't keep pace with, carrots, Jerusalem artichokes, reproachful turnips, beetroots or monstrous regiments of celery, disintegrating under the attack of vitamin-hungry slugs. If you don't have a vegetable garden you can still make use of gluts, and when the whole market is suddenly flooded with cheap tomatoes, that is the time to make tomato soup.

The beauty of a very humble soup, like carrot or turnip, or of any home-made soup in fact, is much more evident if you don't plonk it onto the table in a saucepan. A traditional china or earthenware soup tureen makes it look ten times more glorious. And having spent only a few pennies on the basic ingredients, the extra expense of a shilling on egg-yolks and cream can lift even quite a boring plain soup into luxuriousness, making it rich and velvety and lustrous, and a great compliment to the cook.

Consommé

2–3 lbs beef or veal shin bones sawn up and with
   some meat on
2 pig's trotters split in four
3 onions
4 carrots
2 stalks celery
bouquet garni
6–7 peppercorns
salt
1 egg white
white wine, lemon juice or sherry (optional)

Consommé is gelatinous stock strong enough to
form a jelly, which has been clarified to make it
specklessly clear. It is useful for all sorts of dishes;
they taste much more interesting with home-made
rather than tinned consommé, and cost much less.
Jellied eggs, a tarragon chicken in jelly, jellied
cream cheese, all need a good stiffish consommé.
Pigs' or calves' feet contribute quite enough gelatine
for a home-made consommé to stand up on its own,
but if the weather is very hot, or you want it even
stiffer than it is, you can add gelatine out of a
packet at the very end. Put the bones and the
pig's trotters in a large pan. Cover with 2 quarts
cold water and bring slowly to the boil. Skim and
add the vegetables cut in pieces, peppercorns and
herbs. Simmer for 3–4 hours, covered; then add
a *little* salt, simmer for another half-hour, strain
and completely cool the stock so that the fat can
be removed to the last speck, and you can see how
strongly jellied your stock is. Return it to the stove
and boil until it is reduced to the required amount
to make it set. A glass of white wine or a dash of
sherry at this stage is a good addition. Drop in
the white of an egg beaten to a soft peak, and whisk
it in. Boil it up until the froth rises in the pan,
remove it from the heat and whisk again. Repeat
the boiling and whisking twice more to make sure
the egg white is cooked. Put a cloth wrung out in
hot water over a colander with a large wire strainer
on top. Pour the stock through. The sediment will
be caught in the egg white leaving the stock crystal
clear. Add more sherry, lemon juice and salt to taste
and heat. It will set to a beautiful jelly when cold.

Chicken Broth with Butter Dumplings

2 pints very good chicken broth
1½ oz butter
1 small egg
1½ oz plain flour
½ oz self-raising flour
salt
chopped parsley
½ teaspoon grated lemon peel

Soften the butter and cream with the egg. Add the
flour (both kinds), salt, parsley and lemon peel.
Add a little more plain flour if the mixture is too
wet. Make little balls the size of a pea with the
mixture. Drop these one by one into the simmering
broth, cover and simmer ten minutes. The dumplings
will swell nicely and be light as a feather.

☐ *These dumplings should be tiny and not at all filling.*

For 4

Egg Soup

½ pint very good clear stock (use chicken or beef
    cube if necessary, or use the consommé recipe,
    page 12)
1 slice crustless white bread
butter
1 egg
1 dessertspoon grated Parmesan if liked

Before you start, heat a soup-plate as much as you
safely can; then, while the bouillon or stock is
heating, fry the piece of bread golden on both sides
in butter. Try to finish it just as the soup comes to
boiling point. Put it quickly on the hot soup plate,
break an egg on to the fried bread and pour the
boiling liquid slowly on to the egg. Let it stand for
three to four minutes before eating. The egg should
be extremely lightly cooked by the combined heat of
the plate, bread and soup. Sprinkle with cheese if
liked.

☐ *A marvellous soup for convalescence or hangovers.*

For 1

Kidney Soup

6 lambs' kidneys
½ oz butter
3 pints very good, but not salty, stock (you can
    improve your stock by boiling with chopped
    onions, carrots and turnips)
2 oz flour
bouquet garni of thyme, parsley and bayleaf
1 blade mace
1 stick celery
6 peppercorns
salt to taste

Skin and halve the kidneys, removing the cores. Fry
them in the butter in a saucepan until well browned,
add the stock and bring gently to simmering point.
Add the bouquet garni, mace, celery and peppercorns. Cover and simmer gently for one hour. Strain
the liquid into a clean saucepan, remove the herbs,
peppercorns and celery, and chop the kidneys
finely.
Mix the flour in a large bowl with a little cold water,
and add the reheated liquid just before it comes to
the boil, stirring carefully to avoid lumps. Return
it to the saucepan (through a sieve if it is lumpy in
spite of everything), add the chopped kidneys and
simmer, stirring, for five to ten minutes. Check
seasoning, and serve with hot toast.

☐ *This is one of the best meat soups, thoroughly
British and very rich.*

For 5–6

Scotch Broth

1 lb neck or breast of lamb
2 carrots
1 onion
2 leeks
½ small cabbage
1 stick celery
1 small turnip or slice of swede
2 tablespoons pearl barley
bunch parsley
salt and freshly ground pepper

Stracciatella

2½ pints good clear chicken stock
2 eggs
2 tablespoons grated Parmesan (optional)
1 tablespoon semolina (optional)

Put the neck or breast of lamb in a large pan and cover with plenty of cold water. Bring to the boil and skim carefully. Throw in another cupful of cold water, bring to the boil and skim again. Simmer the meat while you clean all the vegetables and chop them small. Throw them and the pearl barley into the pan with the meat, add salt, pepper and half the parsley, and simmer gently, covered, for about two hours.

Remove the meat (if it is breast you can use it for epigrams, page 113) and keep it hot to eat with a caper sauce. Sprinkle a handful of freshly chopped parsley into the soup, taste for seasoning and serve.

☐ *A great, filling winter soup.*

For 4–6

Beat the eggs very well and add the cheese and semolina. Dilute with a cupful of cold stock. Heat the rest of the well-seasoned stock and as it approaches the boil gently pour in the egg mixture. Stir it with a fork in a clockwise direction rather fast. Turn the heat really low and leave the soup slowly spinning for two to three minutes. Ideally the egg should form long, thin soft threads, but more often it looks like yellow snowflakes; never mind, it tastes the same.

☐ *A very good soup for convalescents and delicate stomachs.*

For 4

Artichoke Soup

2 lbs Jerusalem artichokes
1 onion, peeled and sliced
parsley
1 pint stock, water or bouillon made with a cube
1 pint milk
nutmeg
salt, freshly ground pepper
butter
croûtons or diced fried bacon

This is a very easily made and delicious soup. The only boring part is peeling the artichokes, and if they have only just come out of the ground you may not have to. But if they are already brown on the outside it is worth taking the trouble to do so as your soup will have an infinitely better colour and flavour. Peel the artichokes and put them immediately into cold water acidulated with a dash of vinegar or lemon juice. Put the sliced onion and artichokes and a bunch of parsley tied with a thread into a large pan, cover with the stock and cook until tender, about 30 minutes. Take out the parsley. Sieve or liquidise finely, stir in the milk, reheat and add a large knob of butter, a grate of nutmeg and salt and pepper as needed. Serve with croûtons or diced fried bacon.

For 4–5

Cabbage Soup

1 large onion
1 oz butter or lard
1 cabbage (about 1 ½ lbs, either white or Savoy)
½ lb soaked haricot beans or 2 cubed potatoes, or ¼ lb haricots and 1 cubed potato
4 cloves garlic, peeled
3 pints fresh stock
large bunch parsley
hefty pinch thyme
salt and freshly ground pepper
2 large skinned tomatoes

Chop the onions and fry in butter or lard in a large, heavy saucepan. Add the chopped cabbage, soaked beans and/or potato cubes, garlic cloves, parsley, thyme and cold stock. Don't add salt yet. Bring it slowly to the boil; skim, and simmer gently, uncovered, for three hours. Add salt, pepper and the skinned, chopped tomatoes 30 minutes before the end. Serve with chopped parsley. It is really a glorious filling sort of stew, brown and very warming.

For 6

Carrot Soup with Oatmeal

2 lbs carrots, scraped and sliced
2 stalks celery, chopped
2 onions, peeled and chopped
2 oz butter
2 teaspoons sugar
2 teaspoons salt
4 pints water or light chicken stock (can be made
    with a bouillon cube)
sprig of thyme
2 oz fine oatmeal
parsley, chopped
thin cream or top of the milk

Melt the butter in a large pan and add the celery, onions and carrots with sugar and salt. Sweat them for a few minutes, stirring, then pour on warm water or stock and add the sprig of thyme. Bring to a quiet simmer, cover and cook for $1\frac{3}{4}$–2 hours. Sieve everything except the thyme into a clean pan. Mix the oatmeal with half a cup of milk or water to a smooth paste in a separate basin; add one or two ladles of the soup to the oatmeal, then stir the oatmeal mixture into the soup, taste for salt and simmer, stirring, for ten minutes. Stir in some cream or top of the milk. Add a sprinkling of parsley to each serving.

For 8

Hot Cucumber Soup

1 small cucumber, peeled
1 medium-sized potato, peeled
4–5 spring onions
$1\frac{1}{2}$–2 pints good chicken stock
butter
salt and freshly ground pepper

Grate the potato and cucumber coarsely; strain off the liquid that forms and put the vegetables to sweat with the finely chopped onions in enough butter to cover the bottom of a medium saucepan. Heat the stock to simmering point and add to the vegetables. Simmer gently for 20–25 minutes. Check seasoning and serve with a knob of butter in each bowl.

☐ *Cucumber used to be eaten hot as often as cold; Eliza Acton recommends this highly, but lots of people have forgotten about it. It tastes quite different cooked, and is strangely interesting.*

For 4

Cold Cucumber Soup

1 cucumber
1 5 oz pot plain yoghurt
milk, straight out of the refrigerator
a couple of sprigs of fresh mint, chopped
salt, freshly ground pepper

In your liquidiser blend the peeled, chopped cucumber and yoghurt. Add enough milk to make up to one and a half pints. Chop the mint by hand and stir it in. Season and chill.

☐ *This is almost too simple if you have a liquidiser, but impossible if not. It is deliciously refreshing on a hot day.*

For 4

Leek Soup

1 lb leeks
1 onion
1½ oz butter
1½ oz flour
2 pints chicken or veal stock
salt and pepper
dash of cream or top of the milk *or* croûtons *or* crisply
    fried bacon

Clean the leeks, leaving as much green as you can, and peel the onion. Chop both as finely as possible, which takes ages. Melt the vegetables in the butter in a large pan for about 15 minutes, stirring often, and without browning. Stir in the flour, allow it to thicken and then add the stock gradually. Season and simmer covered until the leeks are tender but still a pleasant green. Serve with croûtons, or a spoonfull of cream or little cubes of crisply fried bacon thrown sizzling into the soup bowls.

☐ *Very filling.*

For 4–6

Lettuce Soup

1 lettuce (keep the heart for sandwiches), or a few
   small lettuces from thinning the rows
1 large onion
1 large potato
½ oz butter
1 ½ pints delicate chicken stock (or stock cube and
   water)
½ pint milk
salt and freshly ground black pepper
1 egg yolk (optional)

Wash the lettuce and break up the leaves; chop the
onion and potato roughly. Melt the butter in a large
pan and soften the lettuce and onion in it without
browning. When they are soft add the potatoes and
the boiling stock. Simmer uncovered for 20–30
minutes until the potatoes are cooked; sieve, mouli
or liquidise for just a few seconds, moistening with
milk. Add the rest of the milk and taste for seasoning. Heat through and serve with hot, well-fried
croûtons. An egg yolk, stirred in at the last moment,
makes a much richer soup.

☐ *You can use sorrel to make this soup, or lettuce and
sorrel together.*

For 4

Pasta e Fagioli

6 oz haricot beans, previously soaked
3 medium potatoes, peeled and cubed
3 sticks celery, cut small
1 fennel root (if available) cut in strips
4 cloves garlic
salt and freshly ground pepper
4 oz short macaroni
parsley, chopped
2–3 tablespoons Parmesan, grated

Put the haricot beans in a large pan with two quarts
of water, bring to the boil and cook gently for one
hour, adding no salt. Then add the vegetables cut
up small and the whole cloves of garlic. Add salt and
pepper and simmer another 20–30 minutes until all
the vegetables are tender, turn up the heat, and
when the soup is gently boiling throw in the
macaroni.

Chop a handful of parsley and throw it with the
grated cheese into the soup as soon as the pasta is
tender. Serve immediately. If the soup seems too
thick, add a little more water. If it is too thin, you
can stir in a couple of tablespoons of mashed potato,
or if this is not available, ladle out some of the
vegetables in the soup, purée them, and return them
to the soup.

For 6–8

Fresh Pea Soup

2 lbs fresh peas
1 bunch spring onions
½ chicken stock cube⎱ or 1 pint fresh chicken stock
1 pint water ⎰
1 pint creamy milk
1 tablespoon cream
few chives, chopped
salt, pepper

Shell the peas and cook them with the chopped spring onions in the stock. When tender, sieve finely or put them through a mouli or liquidiser. Add the milk and heat through. Season. Serve with a tablespoon of cream and a sprinkling of chopped chives on each bowl. This is also good cold.

☐ *An absolutely simple and easy soup, delicate and a pretty pale green.*

For 4

Spanish Soup

1 onion, 4 small leeks
1 small aubergine
3 small potatoes
½ pint stock
2–3 tomatoes
2 small red or green sweet peppers
4 oz French beans
2 cloves garlic
few sprigs parsley
pinch sweet paprika
olive oil, salt

Chop the peppers into one-inch squares, removing every seed. Simmer in oil for 30 minutes. Slice the onion across and quarter it. Cut the cleaned leeks into half-inch pieces. Cut the aubergine into cubes and sprinkle these with salt. Set them to drain. Start cooking the onions and leeks in a pan with 1½ pints cold water. Cube the potatoes and add them after 15 minutes with ½ pint stock. Taste for seasoning. Skin and chop the tomatoes; add them to the soup after twenty minutes with the peppers, the rinsed aubergines and the beans broken in pieces. Cook until the beans are tender, then season again if necessary. Sprinkle chopped garlic and parsley and a large pinch of paprika into each plateful of soup.

This is a very adaptable soup. If you haven't got beans, leave them out; if you have courgettes, put them in; if you have marvellous fresh cabbage, put in a few good inner leaves, cut up. In Spain it is a real stand-by and they regard it as quick to make, which may explain why lunch is never ready until three o'clock.

For 2–3

Lemon Spinach Soup

1 small onion or shallot
1 lb spinach
1½ pints stock
½ lemon
2 egg yolks
salt
handful rice (optional)

Chop the onion finely and the spinach coarsely.
Simmer in the stock, uncovered, for about 20
minutes until tender. Sieve or put through a mouli.
Pour the soup back into the pan. Beat the egg yolks
in a bowl and add two tablespoons of the hot (not
boiling or even simmering) soup. Add this to the
soup in the pan with the juice of half a lemon.
Season and heat very, very gently but don't simmer
or it will curdle. Serve very hot.
No garnish is necessary.
If you want a more filling soup you can add a handful of rice, boiled and still hot, with the egg and
lemon juice.

For 4

Tomato Soup

1½ lbs tomatoes
½ oz butter, dash of oil
1 medium potato, peeled and chopped
1 medium onion, peeled and sliced
2 teaspoons sugar
1 teaspoon salt
1½ pints water
sprig of parsley
bayleaf, or, if available, some basil
1 tablespoon tomato purée (optional)

Chop the tomatoes roughly but leave the skins on.
Melt the butter in a saucepan with the oil and cook
the potato and onion until they start to soften.
They tend to stick so stir them with a wooden spoon.
Add the tomatoes and let them soften. Add salt,
sugar, pepper, herbs and water. Simmer uncovered
until the potatoes are cooked. Remove the bayleaf,
and sieve, mouli or liquidise everything else. Reheat
just before serving, correct seasoning. Add tomato
purée if it is too pale, which will depend a lot on the
tomatoes you use. Anyway it won't be a fierce
orange like tinned tomato soup but a much prettier
soft orangey red. Stir a little cream into each plate
as you serve it.

☐ *This soup is much more delicate than it sounds.*

For 6

Turnip Soup

5 medium turnips, peeled and coarsely chopped
2 tablespoons butter
1 large onion, finely chopped
2–3 pints boiling water
4–5 slices bread
2 egg yolks
¼ pint thin cream or top of the milk
salt, freshly ground pepper

Cook the turnips and onion in butter, in a large
pan, until they start to soften, but not to brown. Add
boiling water and seasoning and crumble in the
bread, crusts removed. Simmer gently until the
vegetables are tender (25–30 minutes). Sieve or
liquidise. Beat the egg yolks with the cream and add
to the re-heated soup, away from the heat. Stir over
a low heat until smooth and creamy, without boiling
or even simmering, and serve with a nut of butter
in each bowl.

For 4–6

Two of Everything Soup

2 medium-sized leeks
2   ,,   ,,   carrots
2   ,,   ,,   potatoes
1½–2 pints boiling water
salt
milk, if necessary
knob of butter
croûtons for garnish, if liked

Into a large saucepan put the potatoes and carrots
cleaned and cut into inch-square pieces, and the
leeks, including all the good green parts, cut in
inch-long slices. Pour on enough boiling water to
cover the vegetables by half an inch. Add ½ teaspoon
salt. Cover the pan and simmer the soup for three-
quarters to one hour, or up to two hours or more
if you want to go out, but it must cook very gently.
Put the soup through the mouli or liquidiser, return
it to the cleaned pan, bring it back to the boil and
simmer it gently for five minutes. If it is too thick
add a little milk; if too thin, cook a little longer. It
should be the consistency of thin cream. Taste for
salt, add a knob of butter and serve plain or gar-
nished with small croûtons of fried bread.

For 4

Vichyssoise

1 lb leeks
2–3 medium potatoes
1 onion
parsley
1 pint chicken stock
1 pint creamy milk
salt and white pepper
chives
thin cream (optional)

Clean and chop the leeks, peel and slice the potatoes and onion. Put the vegetables in a pan with the parsley tied in a bundle, and cover with the stock. Simmer until all the vegetables are tender. Remove the parsley, then sieve the vegetables, helping them through the sieve or mouli (finest disc) by moistening with milk. Add the rest of the milk, just enough to make a thinnish creamy soup, season with salt and a little freshly ground white pepper, and chill. Serve cold with chopped chives and a thread of cream if you have it. This tastes very good hot if the weather suddenly turns cold.

☐ *A well-known mid-Atlantic soup.*

For 4

Watercress Soup

2 bunches watercress
2–3 large potatoes
1 onion
1½ pints stock (or stock cube and water)
1 pint milk
salt and freshly ground pepper
knob of butter

Put the potatoes and onion, peeled and roughly chopped, into a large pan. Add cold stock, bring to the boil and simmer for 15–20 minutes; now throw in the washed watercress, stalks and all, and cook until it is tender but still a good green. Sieve all this, helping it through the mouli by moistening with the milk. If you want a green-flecked soup, use a coarse disc for your mouli; if a uniform green, use a finer disc. You can do either with a liquidiser by adjusting the timing. Now add enough milk to make the soup a good consistency. Return the soup to the stove, season and heat through. Serve with a nut of butter and a sprig of watercress in each plate.
If you sweat the watercress and onion in butter before adding the potato and stock, you make a slightly richer soup. The watercress looks best very coarsely chopped to make large green flecks.

For 6

Chick Pea Soup

6–8 oz chick peas
olive oil
1 clove garlic, chopped
1 onion, peeled and sliced
1 green pepper, de-seeded and chopped
3 anchovy fillets, chopped
3 tomatoes, skinned and chopped
pinch rosemary
4 oz short macaroni (or long macaroni broken up)
salt

Soak chick peas overnight, or all day. Put in a large pan, cover with plain cold water and bring slowly to the boil. Simmer gently, adding more boiling water if necessary, for two to three hours until tender. Add no salt yet. Cover the bottom of a sauté pan with olive oil and sauté the onions, garlic, peppers and anchovies over a moderate heat until tender. Add the tomatoes and a pinch of chopped rosemary. Simmer five or ten minutes more, then add this mixture to the chick peas and their liquid. Season with salt at this point and bring to the boil. Add the macaroni and cook the soup until the macaroni is tender. It should taste as though it is made with a really good beef-broth — the anchovies, though they seem to disappear completely, make this contribution to the soup.

☐ *This is a coarse soup with a marvellous earthy flavour.*

For 4

Dutch Pea Soup

1 lb dried peas (split green ones)
1 knuckle green bacon, soaked overnight
1 fresh pig's trotter (if salt, soak overnight)
2 onions, peeled and chopped
2 leeks, cleaned and cut up
2–3 sticks celery
4–5 frankfurters
butter for frying

Soak the peas for two to four hours. Take a large saucepan and put in the drained peas; cover with six pints water, and simmer, covered, without salt for one or two hours. Add the bacon and pig's trotter and simmer two hours more. In a separate pan soften the fresh vegetables in butter while you sieve or liquidise the pea soup, having first removed the meat to a plate. Add the softened vegetables to the puréed pea soup and cook on for an hour more, over a very low heat. Stir from time to time to prevent it from catching. Leave, covered, overnight. Next day chop the meat from the knuckle into small pieces, and add it with the sliced frankfurters to the soup, which should have set solid. Heat through, taste for seasoning, and if the pea-starch, which expands, has made it too thick, add a little water. You can adjust the amount of bacon and sausages to the number of people and their appetites. The pig's foot is thrown out, but it does a lot for the texture of the soup and adds nourishment.

☐ *This soup is very filling and can be eaten as a meal on its own. It is best if made the day before.*

For 6–8

Lentil Soup

½ lb green lentils
2 pints water or beef stock
1 onion
1 stick celery
4 cloves garlic
salt and freshly ground pepper
butter
1–2 potatoes, cubed

Soak the lentils overnight. Bring them slowly to the boil in the water or stock, and skim. In a separate pan soften the finely chopped onion, garlic and sliced celery in a little butter. Add the lentils in their boiling stock and the potato cubes. Season with salt and pepper. Simmer gently until the lentils are cooked, about one hour. The soup should be a rich dark brown and is very filling.

For 4

Cockle Chowder

2 quarts cockles, well washed and scrubbed
4 rashers bacon, cut small
1 oz butter
1 Spanish onion, chopped
2–3 parboiled floury potatoes, cut into cubes
¾ pint milk (or up to 1 pint)
handful chopped parsley
freshly ground pepper

Take a large pan with a lid and bring about an inch of water to the boil in it. Throw in the cockles, put on the lid and leave over a high flame. Shake the pan from time to time, or stir the cockles once or twice with a wooden spoon; after four to five minutes all the shells should be open and the cockles slightly cooked. Remove all the shells, put the cockles aside and strain the liquid through a cloth. In another pan melt one ounce of butter, let the pieces of bacon sizzle in it, add the onion and cook gently until it is transparent. Add the potatoes, ¾ pint of the strained cockle liquid, and the milk. Let this simmer very gently until the potatoes are soft but not a total mush. Add the shelled cockles, pepper and parsley; heat thoroughly but gently, and test for saltiness (it should not need any extra salt as the cockle liquid is salty, and so is the bacon).
Serve with thick, hard ships' biscuits. Lovers of *Moby Dick* might break their biscuits into the soup. Water biscuits or crackers will do.

☐ *An English seaside version of clam chowder.*

For 4

Italian Cockle Soup

2 quarts cockles, fresh and very well washed
¾ pint water
¼ pint olive oil
1 clove garlic, chopped fine
small handful parsley, chopped fine
2–3 anchovy fillets, chopped
1 tablespoon tomato purée diluted in ¼ pint water,
    or ¼ pint fresh tomato sauce
small glass white wine
oregano
4 slices bread, fried crisp in olive oil at the last
    minute

Open the cockles by boiling fast, covered, in a large
pan with ¾ pint water. Shake the pan a couple of
times and remove the cockles when they have all
opened. Strain the liquid scrupulously through a
damp cloth, while you prepare the rest of the soup.
In another large pan heat the oil, add garlic, parsley,
anchovies and wine. Let it simmer five minutes, add
the tomato purée, diluted, or tomato sauce, and
simmer gently four or five minutes more. Add the
cockles, most of their shells removed as they clutter
up the plate rather, the oregano and the strained
liquid, and simmer three to four minutes more while
you put one slice of hot, golden, fried bread in each
soup plate. Pour the soup, shells and all, over the
fried bread and serve straight away. You probably
will not need salt as the cockles exude sea water.

□ *This soup has a good pungent Mediterranean
flavour. You can make it very well with mussels if
cockles are not available.*

For 4

Fish Soup (Velouté d'Eperlans)

1 pint milk, infused with a sliced onion and a bayleaf
1 slice home-made type white bread
1 oz butter
1 medium onion, finely chopped
1 lb skinned fillets lemon sole, plaice or whiting
4 oz smelts
½ pint thin Béchamel sauce (page 178)
pinch cayenne pepper
salt
chives

Cut the crusts off the bread and pour on a little of
the strained hot milk. Pound to a paste (*panada*),
gradually adding the rest of the milk. Add the
chopped onion, cayenne and salt. Poach the fish
fillets in this for 30 minutes. Don't worry if it looks
odd at this stage. Meanwhile make the Béchamel
and stew the cleaned smelts in 1 oz butter without
browning them. Sieve the *panada* mixture, or pass
through the mouli with the flesh from the smelts
and the butter in which they were cooked. Help the
mixture through with extra milk if it gets too dry.
Add the sieved mixture to the Béchamel sauce and
mix in thoroughly. Season and heat through. If the
soup is too thick, add extra milk.
Serve with chopped chives on top.

□ *The smelts have a very strong flavour, cucumbery
and odd; use very few or they will be overpowering.*

For 4

Smoked Haddock Soup

1 smoked medium-size haddock (about 12 oz)
water
1 onion, chopped and peeled
1 pint milk
few tablespoons mashed potato (better made
    specially for the soup — use 2 potatoes)
½ oz butter
salt and freshly ground pepper
parsley

Skin the haddock, and set the skin aside. Put the
haddock in a shallow pan and pour on enough
boiling water to cover. Bring slowly to the boil, then
add the chopped onion. When the haddock is just
tender remove it from the pan, take the flesh off the
bones and flake it. Put the bones and skin back in
the pan and simmer, covered, for one hour. When
the skin, bones and onion have thoroughly flavoured
the stock, strain it, bring it to the boil again, and
add the milk, brought to the boil in a separate pan,
and the flaked fish. Slowly add enough mashed
potato to give the soup a creamy consistency. At
the last moment taste for salt and pepper and stir
in the butter. Serve sprinkled with chopped parsley,
or put another lump of butter in each bowl.

For 4

Moules Marinières

1 or 2 quarts mussels, depending on how greedy
    you are
2 oz butter
1 medium onion, finely chopped
1 clove garlic (if liked)
small glass white wine
handful of fresh parsley, finely chopped
freshly ground pepper

Scrape, scrub and thoroughly clean the mussels
under running cold water. Throw away any which
float, or are open or damaged. Melt the butter and
fry the onion gently in a capacious saucepan with a
well-fitting lid; add garlic as and if you like. When
the onion is transparent, after about 15 minutes,
grind in some pepper and pour in a small glass of
white wine; let it bubble a minute. Now add the
mussels and slam on the lid, turning up the heat as
high as it will go. Shake the pan once or twice, and
after about four or five minutes, look. It is ready if
all the shells are wide open. Ladle the mussels, as
they are, into a hot china tureen. Strain the now
considerable amount of liquid over them carefully,
because in spite of your cleaning it may still be
gritty. Sprinkle chopped green parsley over the
shiny black-blue shells and serve, providing another
dish for empty shells. It should need no salt if the
mussels are fresh and have recently been living in
the sea.
If you find your own mussels do make sure they
aren't living near a drain. Soak them for a couple of
hours in fresh water, or their liquid will be much too
salty to drink in the soup.

☐ *This is very simple.*

For 2

Eggs and Cheese

It is a long time since everybody living in the country had a coop of laying hens in the orchard, and foxes and broodiness were genuine threats to the family egg supply. Eggs, packed in their own beautiful fragile shells, are abundant, and farms with a quarter of a million chickens apiece keep the poor birds laying night and day. Luckily, although one may not approve of chickens being treated as egg-laying units, the massive production methods and subsidies do mean that eggs stay comparatively cheap, and therefore it is worth being lavish with them; they are such an incredibly unwasteful way of handing out first-class protein, and after all, a really perfect soufflé is just as much of a treat as a fresh salmon trout or a fillet of beef, and is very much easier to make than people suppose.

It is probably worth buying large eggs for eating and small eggs to use in cooking, for cakes, sauces, and for brushing the tops of pies and so on. Otherwise this can be wasteful, though both yolks and white can be kept in the refrigerator, covered with foil. Eggs in their shells do not have to be kept in the refrigerator. They are so beautiful and they get eaten up so quickly, it is surely more sense to keep them somewhere they can offer the cook a bit of inspiration; anyway, lots of sauces can't easily be made with a chilled egg.

One of the greatest companions for eggs is cheese. We are only concerned here with cheese for cooking, and the recipes use a tremendous amount of Parmesan and Swiss Emmenthal, or Gruyère, which is similar but with smaller and less frequent holes. These are not the cheapest cheeses there are by any means, but they are invaluable in the kitchen because they cook so well, and keep for weeks, scarcely suffering at all; however dry they get they can still be used for grating. Keep them wrapped in greaseproof paper in the larder or refrigerator. Many Italian provision shops and delicatessens sell Parmesan, but if the price really staggers you, there are cheaper, slightly stronger, versions of it: Pecorino Romano, which is called Vacchino Romano when made with cow's milk, and Caprino Romano when made with goat's milk, and Sardo which is the same cheese but made in Sardinia. It really is an extravagance to buy ready-grated

Parmesan in little pots; not only does it cost more, but it tastes terrible. If you cannot go often to an Italian supplier, invest in a really large lump of one of the grating cheeses: it is worth the pain of momentary extravagance.

Good cooking cheeses, which can always be substituted for the imported ones if necessary, are Cheddar and Cheshire (or Chester as the French call it). Fresh Mozzarella, which is referred to in one or two recipes, is another Italian cheese, soft and round and white, which traditionally was made with buffaloes' milk, but now probably only of cows' milk, and which should be stored in a bowl of cold water in the refrigerator. It is dull on its own, but wonderful with a salad or cooked, when it becomes rich and succulent. If it is not available, Bel Paese is a fairly good substitute.

Scrambled Egg

It was Boulestin who raised scrambled egg from a humble breakfast dish to the sort of food you could offer your friends and guests. He was right: there is nothing more delicious than *well* scrambled egg and there are lots of variations on the plain creamy golden sort that one eats when alone in the house.

How to cook scrambled egg, if you haven't already got a perfect method. Melt a large lump of butter in a saucepan, add as many lightly beaten eggs as you need, seasoned with salt and pepper, and stir continuously with a wooden spoon over a medium to low heat until you have a pan of creamy eggs. Take it off the heat just before you think it is set as it goes on cooking, by its own heat and that of the pan, for a few seconds.

Variations on Scrambled Egg

Make scrambled egg as usual and before it sets add one of the following:

(1) cold cooked salmon, flaked
(2) cold cooked smoked haddock, flaked
(3) grated cheese or cheese cut in little squares
(4) mussels, cockles or fresh shrimps, cooked and shelled
(5) anchovies previously soaked in milk and drained
(6) chopped tarragon or chives or a combination of parsley, chives and chervil
(7) skinned chopped tomato, first grilled whole
(8) chopped ham or tongue

or

before adding to the scrambled egg, cook one of the following in butter:

(1) sliced button mushrooms
(2) chopped chicken livers
(3) cubes of bacon
(4) cubes of cooked potato
(5) skinned diced lambs' kidneys
(6) chopped spring onions

or serve plain scrambled egg

(1) in an open, buttered and seasoned baked potato
(2) on a bed of spinach

or make a Pipérade (opposite)

Pipérade

2 medium onions
2 cloves garlic
3 tablespoons oil
2 red peppers
4 tomatoes, skinned
4 eggs
salt and freshly ground pepper

Melt the sliced onions in the oil in a heavy pan, add the crushed cloves of garlic and cook gently, without browning, for 15 minutes. Meanwhile slice up the peppers, removing all the seeds, add them to the onions, and cook on without browning until the peppers are tender. Chop the tomatoes and add them to the stew. Add a little salt and simmer on for about 25 minutes until the mixture is moist but not wet. Now beat the eggs lightly in a bowl, season with salt and pepper and stir them into the vegetables as you would for scrambled eggs. When the eggs begin to thicken, it is cooked. Serve it in a plain earthenware dish with triangles of fried bread, or have mounds of fresh bread and butter on the table.

☐ *This was originally a dish eaten by Basque sailors; it is both rich and simple.*

For 4

To make Baked Eggs

First method — straightforward and foolproof
Heat the oven to Reg 4/350°. Butter the cocottes and season with salt and freshly ground pepper before you put the eggs in. Put a baking tin half full of water to warm up on top of the cooker. Gently lower the cocottes with their eggs into the hot water and go on gently heating until the eggs look cloudy at the bottom. Then put the whole thing in the centre of the oven for 15–20 minutes, while you gently heat some seasoned cream in a pan. See if the eggs are set, and if so take them out of the oven and put them on to plates before pouring the hot cream on them. This way you can be sure they are neither under- nor overcooked because you can see the eggs.

Second method — quicker but less foolproof
Heat the oven to Reg 4/350°. Butter the cocottes and break an egg into each. Pour on enough cream to cover each egg completely. Season with salt and freshly ground pepper, and place in the oven. After 15 minutes keep looking at the eggs and shaking them to see if they are cooked. When the white under the cream just won't shiver, but before it is solid, they are cooked.

One or two per person

To Poach an Egg

Shallow pan of boiling salted water with a tablespoon
    of vinegar or lemon juice in it
Eggs (very fresh)

First method
When the water, about two inches deep, is boiling
in the pan, turn it down to a perceptible simmer and
break an egg, sliding it into a nice still part of the
pan. With a spoon keep the white together. Let it
simmer until completely opaque. Lift out carefully
with a slotted spoon.

Second method
When the water, about three inches deep, is boiling,
whirl it round gently with a spoon or fork, and if
nervous break the egg into a cup before you put it in
the water. When the egg hits the water the strands
of egg white will neatly spin round the yolk with the
action of the water. It will sink to the bottom of the
pan but rise to the surface as it cooks. Lift it out
with a slotted spoon after three to four minutes.
Drain well.

To cook more than one egg
Use a larger pan, break them all into one bowl and
slip the whole lot into the water at once. Lift out
gently one at a time, or two by two and separate
them when you have them on a plate or dish. Drain
well.

Oeufs Bénédictine

4 eggs, poached

For Hollandaise (*page* 179)
2 extra yolks
squeeze lemon juice
4 oz butter
salt and pepper
4 large tablespoons smoked haddock purée (page 71)
4 rounds fried bread

Spread a layer of haddock purée on each piece of
fried bread, put a poached egg on top and pour the
Hollandaise sauce over. Serve straight away. This
was originally made with salt cod, never with ham
(though that can be nice too), as it was a Lenten
dish.

For 4

Oeufs en Gelée

4 eggs
½ pint jellied home made consommé (page 12) or
  one tin consommé
2 tablespoons sherry, if there is none in the
  consommé
2 slices smoked ham
tarragon or flat (Greek or German) parsley

Oeufs Mollets aux Fines Herbes

1 (or 2) egg(s) for each person
½ oz butter per egg
3 or 4 twigs tarragon
3 or 4 sprigs parsley or, better still, chervil
bunch of chives
salt and freshly ground pepper

Stir the sherry into the melted consommé.
In a separate pan poach the eggs carefully (opposite). The yolks should still be runny, otherwise the results will be very disappointing. When they are cooked add half a pint of cold water to the pan to prevent them cooking any more, unless you are ready to use them immediately, in which case lift them carefully out of the water and drain them a little. Trim off the rough outside edges. Lay half a slice of ham, folded up, in the bottom of each of four cocottes. Lay a trimmed egg carefully on to each. Lay the tarragon leaves or parsley in a pattern on top of each egg and pour in enough consommé to come just over the top of each egg. Let them set in a cool place. Some people put pâté in the bottom instead of ham but this can be rather sickly.

☐ *Make these the day before you want to eat them.*

For 4

Bring a pan of water to a steady boil, put in the eggs, which should be at room temperature, not straight out of the fridge, and boil them for exactly five and a half minutes, six for large eggs. Remove and hold under the cold tap until they are cool enough to handle. Tap the shell of each egg carefully all over. Peel with great concentration or large chunks of the white will come zipping out and the egg will sag and crack. When the eggs are shelled they should be soft but not so soft that they break open. Keep them warm in a bowl of warm water.
Melt the butter but don't let it sizzle or start to brown, Strip the tarragon leaves off the stalks and chop the herbs together finely. Stir them into the butter, add a little salt and pepper and pour it over the drained eggs. Serve hot. They won't be absolutely scalding hot, they aren't meant to be.

For 2–4

To Make an Omelette

2 or 3 eggs
salt and pepper
butter

Beat the eggs lightly in a bowl with a little salt and pepper. You can add a tablespoon of water but it is not essential to a good omelette. Melt a large hazelnut of butter in a steel omelette pan used only for its proper purpose. Swirl the butter round to coat the bottom and sides of the pan, and when it starts to brown pour in the eggs at once. Keep a wooden fork or spoon to make omelettes, as a metal one would spoil the surface of the pan. Over a medium heat stir the centre of the omelette briefly. Then, tipping the pan this way and that, lift the setting sides of the omelette to let the uncooked egg on top get to the heat. When there is no more uncooked egg give the pan a short brisk jerk to loosen the omelette, tip to start it rolling over, and help it with your fork; roll it out of the pan on to the middle of a warm plate. It should be plump and juicy and not very brown.

For 1

Omelette Arnold Bennett

1 smoked haddock on the bone (about 1 lb)
½ pint milk
½ pint water
3 oz butter
1½ oz flour
2 oz Parmesan, Emmenthal or Cheddar cheese, grated
salt and freshly ground pepper
8 eggs

Trim tail and collar bones from the haddock and poach gently in half a pint each of milk and water, until the bones come away easily. Make a thick Béchamel sauce with the flour, half the butter and the cheese, using some of the liquid in which the fish has cooked. There should be about half a pint of thickish sauce. Bone the fish and put the flaked pieces into the sauce, reserving about three table-spoons of sauce. Season with pepper and add salt if necessary. Keep it warm while you beat the eggs lightly with a little salt and pepper. Fold the fish mixture into the eggs.

Preheat the grill and a serving dish. Heat the remaining butter in a thick heavy frying pan, tipping it from side to side until it is just starting to brown. Gently pour in the mixture, using the reserved sauce to make a pattern on the top of the omelette, rather like a hot cross bun. Cook gently, allowing the uncooked egg to reach the heat by lifting the omelette carefully and tipping the pan.

When it is set underneath, but still undercooked on top, sprinkle with more cheese and put under a hot grill until the top is just a little brown here and there. Slide it on to a large heated dish, not too hot or the omelette will go on cooking, and serve at once, cut in slices like a cake. The top and bottom should be firmly set and the inside still juicy and slightly runny.

For 4 (main course), or 8 (first course)

Omelette in an Overcoat

8 eggs
½ lb mushrooms
3 oz butter
¼ pint single cream
salt and freshly ground black pepper
1 oz flour
½ pint milk
1 oz Parmesan, freshly grated
2 oz Gruyère, freshly grated

Slice the mushrooms and cook them in two ounces of the butter. Add the cream, salt and plenty of freshly ground pepper and reduce until the mixture thickens. Keep the mushrooms warm while you make a cheese sauce with the remaining butter, flour, milk, salt, pepper and cheese; a dribble of cream kept from the quarter pint could well go into this sauce, it makes it brown so beautifully. With the eight eggs, beaten lightly and seasoned, make a very large omelette into which you put the creamy mushroom filling. Fold the omelette on to a hot (but not very hot) serving plate and pour the cheese sauce all over it. Put the omelette under a hot grill for a minute or two and watch it. When it is a beautiful brown serve it immediately with a green salad.

For 4

Onion and Potato Omelette

6 eggs
salt and pepper
4 potatoes
1 medium onion
butter and oil, for frying

Peel and boil the potatoes. Chop the onion finely and soften in very little oil and butter without browning. Add the cubed cooked potatoes and heat them thoroughly, even brown them a bit. Beat the eggs briefly with salt and pepper, make the omelette as usual and add the potato and onion mixture, spreading it all over, half-way through the cooking. Cook on as usual and serve with a green salad.

☐ *This is a sort of tortilla but it requires fewer potatoes and more eggs than the real thing, and is cooked less fiercely and in far less oil than is used in Spain.*

For 4

Soufflé Cheese Omelette

8 eggs
1 oz flour
1 oz butter
½ pint milk
salt and freshly ground pepper
2 oz Emmenthal cheese, grated
2 oz Parmesan cheese, grated
top of the milk
butter for cooking the omelette

Make a thickish cheese sauce with the butter, flour, milk and grated cheese; add a little top of the milk and seasoning and beat the sauce well until it is glossy. Separate the egg yolks from the whites; beat the whites until they are fluffy. Preheat the grill and a serving dish. Beat the yolks with a little salt and pepper. Heat a tablespoon of butter in a large frying pan, swirling it over the sides and bottom to prevent the omelette from sticking. Rapidly fold the whites into the yolks and when the butter starts to brown slip the mixture into the pan. Let it cook over a moderate heat without stirring until set and golden brown underneath. Then put the pan under the grill for a minute or two. Slide the omelette on to the hot dish, folding it in half. Pour the sauce over it and put it back under the grill to brown quickly. Serve straight away. The omelette should be fluffy inside and the sauce creamy and rich. Eat with a green salad.

☐ *This is a very good main course; it isn't heavy but it is filling.*

For 4

Cheese Soufflé

1½ oz butter
1 oz flour
scant ½ pint milk
3 oz cheese, grated
3 egg yolks and 4 whites
salt and cayenne pepper

Preheat the oven to Reg 7/425°. Prepare a soufflé dish five or six inches in diameter, by buttering liberally and then coating the inside with flour, shaking out any excess.
Make a Béchamel with the butter, flour and milk. Now add the cheese, stirring all the time. Season with salt and cayenne pepper, remove from the heat and beat in the egg yolks one at a time. This mixture should be left off the heat, but somewhere quite warm, while you beat the egg whites to a firm snow. Add one tablespoon of whites to the sauce and stir it in, then fold in the remaining egg whites, add more salt and cayenne pepper if necessary, and turn lightly into the soufflé dish. Put in the oven, turn down the heat to Reg 6/400° and bake 20–25 minutes. Serve straight away while it is brown and puffy and light. Soufflés are definitely better a bit sloppy inside than dry and overcooked. They are nowhere near as sensitive as people think and it is really quite difficult to make a failure. The most frequent disaster is that no one is ready and waiting when the soufflé is just right and it either collapses while it hangs about, or gets overcooked in the oven. There is only one answer and that is to have everyone at the table, forks in hand.

For 4

Little Tomato Soufflés

6 really large tomatoes
1 oz flour
1 oz butter
2 tablespoons cream
1 tablespoon Parmesan, grated
4 eggs plus one white
salt, freshly ground pepper

Preheat the oven to Reg 7/425°. Cut the tomatoes in half and scoop out the insides. Simmer the juice and pulp for a few minutes in a small pan. Sieve and use this purée, seasoned with a little salt and pepper, to make a stiffish sauce with the butter, flour, cream and grated Parmesan. When the sauce has cooled a little, stir in four egg yolks, one at a time, beating each one in well. Beat the five egg whites to a soft light foam. Beat two tablespoons of this into the tomato mixture, and then add the rest, folding it in carefully. Dry the insides of the tomato halves, season and fill them to the top with the mixture. Put into the hot oven. After five minutes turn the heat down to Reg 6/400°. The little soufflés take 15–20 minutes to cook and should be light brown on top. They make a very nice summer lunch dish.

For 6

Smoked Haddock Soufflé

1 small smoked haddock on the bone — approx.
   ¾ lb
½ pint milk
½ pint water
knob of butter
1½ oz flour
2 oz butter
4 eggs plus 1 egg white
1 oz Parmesan, freshly grated
1 oz Gruyère, freshly grated
salt and freshly ground pepper

Preheat oven to Reg 6/400°. Cook the haddock in the milk and water with a knob of butter for ten minutes. Do not let it catch on the bottom of the pan; it is a good idea to cook it skin side up. When it is cooked, strain off the liquid and keep half a pint. Flake the haddock, removing the skin and bones, and chop finely with a knife or flake very small. Make a thick sauce with the flour, butter and half a pint of the haddock liquid, and beat in the grated cheese, keeping a tablespoon or so of Parmesan on one side. Add the haddock, and remove from the heat. Beat in the egg yolks one by one and season the sauce with salt if necessary, and plenty of pepper. Butter a three pint soufflé dish and dust the inside with grated cheese. If you use a large dish you don't have to fiddle with paper collars etc.
Beat the egg whites stiffly. Stir a quarter into the haddock mixture, fold in the rest with a palette knife, turn into the soufflé dish, levelling out the top, and put straight into the oven.
Turn the heat down to Reg 5/375° and bake 25–30 minutes until very brown and puffy. Eat it the instant it is out of the oven, with a green salad. It makes a perfect lunch.

☐ *Smoked haddock combines exceptionally well with eggs, and this is one of the best soufflés of all.*

For 3–4

Egg Croquettes

1½ oz butter
1½ oz flour
½ pint milk, previously infused with a sliced onion,
    6 peppercorns and a bayleaf
4 hard-boiled eggs
flour
1 beaten egg
dried breadcrumbs
salt, freshly ground pepper, and a pinch of nutmeg
oil for deep frying
bacon (optional)

Make a stiff Béchamel with the butter, flour and flavoured milk. Peel the hard-boiled eggs and sieve the yolks into the sauce. Add the whites, coarsely chopped, season well and add a good pinch of nutmeg. Run a china plate under the cold tap for a few seconds, then spread the Béchamel on it and leave it covered in a cool place overnight or for several hours. It should set firmly enough to roll into small cork shapes (about 12 rolls 2 ins. long). Roll these in flour, dip in beaten egg and then coat with breadcrumbs. Deep fry in oil, drain on kitchen paper, and serve very hot either on their own or with tomato sauce (page 185).
You can put chopped bacon, lightly fried, into the mixture with the chopped, hard-boiled egg.

☐ *These ideally should be made a day ahead as the mixture becomes easier to handle after standing several hours.*

For 4

Eggs in a Nest

1½ lbs potatoes
milk, nutmeg, butter
salt, freshly ground pepper } for mashed potatoes
cheese, grated
8 eggs
butter

Peel and cut the potatoes in pieces. Boil them until tender in salted water. Sieve or mash, using plenty of *hot* milk and butter. When they are light and fluffy, season with salt, pepper and a pinch of nutmeg. Add two tablespoons of grated cheese if the children like it. Butter a shallow oven dish of glass or china, put in the mashed potatoes and make eight depressions with the back of a spoon. Gently break an egg into each hollow and sprinkle with a little more grated cheese and some small pieces of butter. Season with a little salt and pepper. Bake at Reg 4/350°, until the eggs are set (10–20 minutes), or bake gently under the grill. Serve at once. The yolks should be runny and the whites firm.

☐ *Very good for children's lunch and for using up mashed potatoes.*

For 4

Eggs in Baked Potatoes

6 eggs
6 large, perfect potatoes
butter
top of the milk or thin cream
salt and freshly ground pepper
freshly grated Parmesan cheese

Bake the potatoes in the oven, Reg $2\frac{1}{2}$/315°, for 2 hours, cool a little and through a hole in the top scoop out enough of the insides to make room for an egg. Put in a knob of butter, salt and pepper. Break an egg into each, add a little cream and Parmesan and bake in a hot oven, Reg 6/400°, for about 15 minutes or until the eggs are set.

☐ *Very good for children's lunch.*

For 6

Eggs in their Dish

2 eggs
1 small onion, chopped
1 tomato, peeled and chopped
salt and freshly ground pepper
oil, butter or bacon fat for frying
additional if liked
1 or 2 rashers of bacon, cut small, *or*
1 sliced cooked potato, *or*
pieces of salami, *or*
pieces of red or green pepper

Use a very small frying pan or enamel gratin dish that you can eat from. Fry the onion (and green pepper if wanted) gently in a teaspoon of fat or oil, until it is transparent but not coloured. (Put the bacon, potato or salami in with the onion.) Peel and chop the tomato. Add it to the onion, season with salt and pepper. Wait until the tomato is beginning to soften but not until it disintegrates. Gently break one or two eggs onto the bed of onion etc. Cook gently. When the bottom is set dot the top with a little butter and finish under a medium grill. The eggs are half poached, half fried and you eat them straight from the dish.

☐ *A very quick lunch if you are by yourself.*

For 1

Fisherman's Toast

4 slices slightly stale white bread, crusts removed
2 eggs, beaten with salt
milk
dripping, butter or bacon fat

Soak the slices of bread in milk, then dip them in the beaten egg. Melt the fat in a large frying-pan and fry the bread slices until golden both sides. Very good for breakfast or supper. A sweet version uses sugar instead of salt; fry in butter or oil and serve sprinkled with sugar, when it is known as *pain perdu*.

☐ *Makes two eggs do for four people.*

For 4 children

Croque Monsieur

2 slices bread
1 slice ham, with not too much fat
1 thin slice Gruyère, with not too many holes
½ oz butter
½ tablespoon oil

Cut the crusts off the bread and thinly butter one side of each slice. Make a sandwich with the slice of ham and slice of Gruyère and press firmly shut. Heat a frying pan with the butter and a dash of oil, and when hot fry the sandwich. Both sides (turn carefully) should be pale gold and the cheese starting to melt; eat at once. It is the French version of Mozzarella in Carrozza (page 41).

For 1

Mozzarella in Carrozza

2 eggs
8 slices home-made type white bread (preferably
    slightly stale)
2 Mozzarella cheeses (or use ¾ lb Bel Paese)
salt and pepper
olive oil

Beat the eggs on a plate with a little salt and pepper.
Soak the bread, cut in three-inch rounds, in the egg
on one side only for about ten minutes. Shake off
the surplus egg.
Cut the Mozzarella into rounds a quarter of an inch
thick. Make thick sandwiches with the cheese and
the soaked bread, eggy side out, and fasten with
toothpicks. Deep fry in olive oil or fry carefully and
not too fast in shallow oil, turning once with great
care. Take out the toothpicks and drain the sandwiches before eating them.
The cheese melts completely inside a crisp brown
crust and when you bite it goes into long strings. In
Italy they are eaten with ham inside and also dipped
in breadcrumbs before they are fried. The simple
thing that can go wrong is that the cheese doesn't
melt but this only happens if the bread is too thick.

☐ *By varying the thickness of the bread you can
make a hefty lunch, or a fairly light start to a meal.*

For 4

Onion, Potato and Anchovy Gratin

2 onions
1 clove garlic, chopped
butter
1 tablespoon olive oil
3 eggs
½ pint milk
1 lb potatoes
10 anchovy fillets
a little cream
salt, if necessary, and freshly ground pepper
cheese (optional)

Make this like the gratin of potatoes and ham
(page 112), but instead of ham and cheese, add the
anchovies and cream to the potato mixture before
you turn it into the gratin dish. Bake as before and
finish under the grill. Go easy on the salt because
of the saltiness of the anchovies.
You can add cheese to this if you like, using the
same quantity as is used in the gratin of ham.

For 4

Egg Curry with Tomatoes
from Harvey Day's
'Curries of India'

6 eggs, 2 oz butter
2 onions, chopped fine
2 cloves garlic, chopped fine
2 green or red chillies (optional)
½ teaspoon ground coriander
½ teaspoon ground cumin
½ teaspoon (or less) ground chilli
¼ teaspoon ground turmeric
3–4 large tomatoes, skinned and chopped
½ oz tamarind (or juice of half a lemon)
salt

Cook this curry in a fireproof dish that you can take to the table. Fry onions, garlic and chillies, de-seeded and cut in strips, in the butter, until lightly browned. Add spices and stir for a minute; add tomatoes and ⅓ pint warm water. Cook slowly for ten minutes. Stir the tamarind into ¼ pint water, soak for five minutes and strain the resulting juice into the tomato sauce, or add lemon juice. Add salt to taste and return to the boil. Gently break the eggs into the sauce. Serve when they are set, after about five minutes. Eat with lots of bread or rice.

☐ *A red-hot chilli and tomato sauce in which you poach the number of eggs you need.*

For 3

Oeufs à la Tripe

6 hard-boiled eggs
½ pint onion sauce (page 182)

Slice the eggs into thick rounds and cover with hot onion sauce. Serve hot.

☐ *This is a good first course.*

For 4

Oeufs à la Soubise

6 hard-boiled eggs
1 lb onions, poached in milk until tender, seasoned and sieved
½ pint creamy, well-flavoured Béchamel (page 178)

Make a mound of onion purée on a hot dish. Place the eggs on top and cover with Béchamel. Serve hot.

For 4

Fromage des Oeufs

12 eggs
salt
1 pint mayonnaise (page 180)
a few anchovies

Cream Cheese Mousse

1 pint consommé (page 12), or 2 tins consommé
8 oz plain cream cheese
2 hard-boiled eggs
salt and freshly ground pepper

Break the eggs into a round flat dish that has been copiously buttered (and lined with buttered grease-proof paper if you want to be extra careful). Be very sure the yolks don't break; although it doesn't spoil the flavour it is not so pretty.

Sprinkle a little salt over the eggs and bake in a bain marie in a slowish oven Reg 3½–4/350°, for 35–40 minutes. Allow to cool, turn out, remove the paper and decorate the top with anchovies in a lattice if you like it to be smart.

Serve the mayonnaise separately.

□ *This is an alternative way of making egg mayonnaise; the eggs come out in a nice shape like a Brie and you cut it like one. This accounts for the name, as there is actually no cheese in it.*

For 6–8

Slice the hard-boiled eggs and lay them in a white soufflé dish. Mix half the consommé, melted, with the cream cheese until it is a smooth cream. Season, pour it into the dish carefully without disturbing the eggs, and chill until firm. Melt the remaining consommé, but it must be cool when you pour it over the cheese mixture, Chill again. It is ready to eat, a pale, creamy mousse with a deep amber layer of consommé on top.

□ *A very good summer lunch dish with a green salad. It is cool, fresh and pale and it doesn't take much of an appetite to eat.*
Make the day before.

For 6

Quiche

1 large onion, finely sliced
1 oz butter
1 teaspoon oil
3 small eggs
½ pint milk
1–2 oz cheese, grated
12 anchovy fillets
salt, if needed, and freshly ground pepper
9 oz flan pastry (page 218)

In the following recipe the filling can be almost anything you like. Instead of onions and anchovies you can put ham or bacon with more cheese; chopped leeks softened in butter, with cheese; cooked crab or shrimps; mushrooms, previously sweated in butter; fresh asparagus with a little cheese; cooked potatoes cut in cubes with ham and chives; a great big panful of softened sliced onions; smoked haddock with a little cheese; or just a really fresh bunch of mixed herbs, finely chopped. Make a flan case (page 217). Keep the oven at Reg 5/375°. Soften the onion in the oil and butter in a small frying pan, without browning. Beat together the eggs, milk and cheese. Put the drained, tender onions in the flan case, lay the anchovies on top and pour on the egg mixture. Bake ten minutes at Reg 5/375°, then another 15–20 at Reg 4/350°. When it is nicely browned and puffed up it is ready. It is better sloppy-ish than overcooked, and pre-cooking the flan case makes sure that the pastry won't be raw. It can be eaten hot or cold, or even tepid, which seems a good temperature for the custard.

For 4 (main course) or 6 (starter)

Onion Tart

¾ lb button onions (about 36 of them)
2–3 rashers bacon, rinds removed
2 eggs
¼ pint single cream or creamy milk
salt, pepper, and a pinch of nutmeg
9 oz flan pastry (page 218), or less if you like a fragile crust

Preheat the oven to Reg 5/375°. Cook a seven-inch flan case (page 217). Trim and peel the little onions, a real labour of love, and cook them whole in boiling salted water for 15–20 minutes. Drain well. Cut the bacon into little strips and fry gently in its own fat. Don't let it become crisp. Arrange the drained onions neatly in the flan case and put little bits of bacon here and there. Beat the eggs with the cream or milk, season with salt, pepper and nutmeg and pour into the tart. Bake it in the moderately hot oven covered with greaseproof paper for 25 minutes; remove the paper and cook five minutes longer to brown the top.
Serve very hot.
If you would rather use larger onions, slice them and sauté them in butter for 30 minutes without browning before putting them into the flan case.

☐ *Made with little, whole, silver or pickling onions as an alternative to ordinary sliced onions.*

For 4–6

Pasta, Pancakes, Gnocchi, Dumplings and Fritters

Packets of spaghetti in their traditional deep blue paper with red and yellow labels are always an encouraging sight in the larder; as long as they are there, preferably lying alongside a large tin of tomatoes and a can of olive oil, you will never be short of a meal. But the truth is that these packets won't keep for years and, especially in the case of noodles, it is better to eat them within a few months of purchasing or you may find yourself serving a bowl of nicely shredded cardboard. Always choose pasta made in Italy — they do know how to do it there — and always cook it with care, it is so boring once it has gone completely soft. The instructions for cooking pasta (page 48) apply to every kind there is from fettucine, tagliatelli and linguine, which are all types of noodles, to macaroni and cannelloni, which are the larger kinds of pasta. Some of the shapes, such as *conchiglie* which are shells and *ruote*, which are wheels, are pretty to have about, but need lots of sauce to make a good dish. Pasta with a sauce, preferably with a heavy aroma of fresh herbs, is a perfect lunch followed by a green salad, cheese and fruit. And if you serve it in the summer on a terrace or under a tree, it can produce a state of euphoria.

Gnocchi are more delicate than pasta and tend to be eaten with less abandon because they cannot be bought but must be freshly made, which seems to give them a touch of luxury although they are a simple form of food. Gnocchi are a wonderful vehicle for sauces and some, such as the green ones, need nothing more than extra butter and Parmesan. They are made with humble ingredients, semolina, potatoes and flour, and so are a very inexpensive meal, but they are rather a fiddle to make.

Pancakes, stuffed with a velvety filling, are a delicious vehicle for the despised left-over; chicken, spinach, smoked haddock, mushrooms, ham, chicken livers, scallops, can each make a good stuffing for a pancake. Bind them in a smooth, not stodgy, well-flavoured sauce, and make the pancakes as thin as possible, light and crisp. As with any other dish that uses left-overs, there is a vital rule to follow: don't be tempted to use more than one in each stuffing. However much you long to get rid of little dishes of sweetcorn and peas sitting neglected in the refrigerator, they will probably bring your pancake down to the mish-mash level.

Dumplings and fritters are often forgotten because they are so plain, and plain cooking is not fashionable. Both are useful and not too taxing ways of extending the possibilities and filling power of ordinary foods, and a stew with light little dumplings swimming in it looks as though somebody really cared about it. Fritters can be quite delicious, especially if made with a very light batter that doesn't hold too much oil (page 60), but it is always vital to drain them really well on kitchen paper. Several vegetables make good fritters; aubergines, courgettes, salsify and sorrel or spinach, dipped a leaf at a time into the egg-white batter, are all excellent. So are mussels, and slices of cheese, not to mention the worthy spam or corned beef fritters, both of which children still admire tremendously.

Cooking Pasta

The difference between pasta cooked well — light, slightly *al dente*, each thread or shape separate — and pasta cooked badly — heavy, glutinous and clinging — is drastic. It's very hard to make a packet of spaghetti that has been hanging about for months taste good, and it *should* always be bought at a shop that sells plenty of it so it is more likely to be fresh. Points to remember if you want to produce a perfectionist dish of pasta:

(1) A teaspoon of butter or oil in the water while the pasta is cooking prevents it from sticking to the pan.

(2) Three ounces of dried pasta is enough for one person.

(3) Ideally you need two gallons of water to cook one pound of pasta, though less will do.

(4) Use one and a half tablespoons of salt to every gallon of water.

(5) Stir the water round before you put the pasta in, and again as soon as the pasta is in, and during the cooking to make sure it doesn't stick together.

(6) Don't overcook the pasta. It should be *al dente*, with a slight resistance when you bite it, so after ten minutes test it every now and then by biting a piece.

(7) When cooked and drained, tip it at once into a large heated dish and stir a little olive oil or butter into it.

(8) Serve it as soon as possible to eat it at its best. If it *must* wait a little while, pour boiling water over it, drain, add butter or oil and keep it warm over a pan of hot water, or in a low oven, covered with a cloth.

(9) Serve most sauces separately and have freshly grated Parmesan and more butter on the table, plus copious amounts of rough red wine. People also like plenty of freshly ground pepper and large chunks of bread.

Freshly-made pasta — if you are lucky enough to get it — is cooked in the same way but for less time; start testing it after eight minutes.

Spaghetti Bolognese

12 oz spaghetti
3 tablespoons olive oil
1 onion, chopped
¾ lb freshly minced beef, pork, or veal and pork
5 tomatoes, skinned and chopped
1 clove garlic
1 tablespoon tomato purée, diluted with a little water
salt and freshly ground pepper
sprig thyme
small bunch parsley
large pinch basil
Parmesan, freshly grated

Heat the oil in a saucepan, peel and chop the onion and sweat in the oil for five minutes without browning. Turn up the heat and, when the oil is very hot, add the meat and fry fiercely to brown it, stirring all the time to keep it crumbly. Peel the tomatoes, chop them coarsely and add to the meat. Chop the clove of garlic finely and add with the diluted tomato purée, salt, freshly ground black pepper and roughly chopped herbs. Cook gently, uncovered, for ¾–1 hour, stirring from time to time. The sauce will condense considerably and should seem bathed in oil and tomato. Serve on pasta (this page), with grated Parmesan as usual, or use in lasagne or cannelloni.

For 4

Spaghetti Carbonara

¼ lb spaghetti or other pasta
3 rashers bacon or slices ham
1 egg
salt and freshly ground pepper
Parmesan, freshly grated

While the pasta is cooking in plenty of boiling water, cut the bacon or ham into thin strips or small squares. Put the rinds or pieces of ham fat into the pan on a low heat and when the fat starts to run take them out and add the bacon or ham strips. Let them cook until the bacon is crisp, or the ham sizzling hot; keep hot. Beat the egg, and season with salt and pepper, unless you know the bacon to be very salty, when you must be very careful with the salt.

When the pasta is ready (15–20 minutes), drain and tip it into a very hot serving dish, then quickly add the beaten egg to the hot pasta and stir it about. Add the bacon or ham and the fat it cooked in. The egg is lightly cooked by the heat of the pasta, but if this seems daunting you can lightly (but very lightly) scramble the egg with the bacon in the pan before pouring it on to the pasta. Sprinkle with cheese, serve more cheese with it at the table. Eat it at once.

☐ *This is useful if you have no tomatoes or other sauce.*

For 2

Spaghetti with Chicken Liver Sauce

12 oz spaghetti
3 tablespoons olive oil
1 onion, chopped
2 cloves garlic
1 ½ lbs tomatoes
parsley, thyme and marjoram, fresh or dried
salt and freshly ground pepper
small glass red wine
¾ lb chicken livers
1 tablespoon butter
Parmesan, freshly grated, if liked

Heat the olive oil in a large shallow saucepan. Chop the onion and garlic and sweat them for 15 minutes in the oil without browning. Skin the tomatoes, chop roughly and add them with the wine, salt, pepper and plenty of chopped herbs, and simmer uncovered for about an hour until you have a thickish sauce. Cook the spaghetti. While it is boiling chop the chicken livers into pieces the size of a hazelnut and sauté in butter for a few minutes until they are brown on the outside. Add them with their juice to the tomato sauce and serve straight away with the spaghetti, with or without grated cheese.

For 4

Spaghetti Alla Puttanesca

12 oz spaghetti
2 red, yellow or green peppers
4 cloves garlic
1–2 oz small black olives
olive oil
Parmesan, freshly grated

Remove every seed from the peppers and cut them into strips. Peel and slice the garlic cloves. Stone the olives if you like. Heat 3–4 tablespoons of olive oil in a sauté pan, and sauté the peppers until they are cooked through, 10–15 minutes. Add the garlic and olives and cook on for three or four minutes, stirring. In the meantime cook the spaghetti in fast-boiling salted water. Drain and put in a large bowl, pour the pepper mixture over and serve with fresh olive oil and grated Parmesan if liked. 'Alla puttanesca' means as a tart would cook it, and it is a very basic dish.

For 4

Noodles with Cockles

¾ lb spaghetti or 1 lb noodles
3 cloves garlic
1 onion, chopped
3 tablespoons olive oil
1 lb tomatoes, skinned, de-seeded and chopped
3–4 sprigs parsley, coarsely chopped
salt and freshly ground pepper
2–3 pints fresh cockles, well washed (pickled ones are horrible)

Chop the garlic and onions and soften in the oil for 15–20 minutes. Add the tomatoes, parsley, salt and pepper and cook a further five minutes. (The tomatoes should be very lightly cooked for this dish.) Meanwhile cook the noodles or spaghetti in plenty of boiling salted water. Shake the well washed cockles in a thick pan over a low heat until they are open, and then remove from their shells. Add them to the sauce at the last minute and heat through. No cheese with this dish unless you are fanatic about it, but you can add more chopped parsley and a dab of butter as you serve it.

For 4

Noodles with Crispy Bacon

1 lb packet egg noodles
4–5 rashers bacon, rinds removed
½ pint cream
2 egg yolks
salt and freshly ground pepper
garlic
Parmesan, freshly grated
chives, chopped

Cook the noodles in boiling salted water until they
are tender but with a bite. Meanwhile fry the bacon
briskly in a dab of butter until it is crisp and brown
but not burned. Beat the egg yolks, chives and
cream together, add the drained bacon, broken
into bits, season if necessary and heat gently in a
double boiler until thick enough to coat the back of
your spoon. You can add a little crushed garlic if
you like. When you have drained the noodles, stir
in the bacon mixture, coating the noodles thoroughly, and serve with grated Parmesan, and more
chopped chives if you like.

☐ *This is an anglicised version of spaghetti carbon-
ara.*

For 4–5

Noodles with Cream and Fresh Herbs

1 lb egg noodles, fresh if possible
¼ pint cream
parsley
chives
rosemary
2 cloves garlic
4 oz butter
salt and freshly ground pepper
Parmesan, freshly grated

Warm the cream. Cook the noodles in boiling salted
water until just tender but with a bite. Drain
thoroughly. Chop the herbs together coarsely. Stir
into the noodles the heated cream, half the butter,
the pounded garlic and chopped herbs, and season
with salt and plenty of ground pepper. Put a tablespoon of grated Parmesan on top of each plateful
of noodles and a good knob of butter on top of that.
A plate of these looks particularly good: creamy
white with green herbs and a yellow pool of butter
in the centre.
As in all spaghetti recipes this sauce can be used on
any kind of pasta, but is best on the thinner, more
delicate kinds: spaghetti, tagliatelle, linguine etc.

For 6, or 4 as a main dish

Lasagne

½ lb lasagne
2 onions
2 cloves garlic
olive oil
¾ lb minced pork
¾ lb minced veal
1 lb tomatoes
salt and freshly ground pepper
thyme
stock if necessary

for the sauce:
3 oz butter
3 oz flour
1½ pints milk
2 oz Parmesan, grated
salt and pepper
bayleaf
grating of nutmeg
butter
cheese for sprinkling on the top

Heat the olive oil in a saucepan and fry the chopped onions and garlic. Add the meat and fry until it is browned, stirring all the time. Skin the tomatoes, chop them roughly and add to the meat with the thyme, salt and pepper. Let the tomatoes soften. If they do not make enough liquid to cook the sauce in, gradually add a little stock, but always a bit less than you think is necessary. Cook the sauce gently, stirring occasionally, for as long as you like, ¾ hour should be enough. Meanwhile cook the lasagne, a few at a time, in a huge pan of boiling well-salted water for 11 minutes, moving them around from time to time to prevent them sticking together. Scoop them out and drain on a cloth.

At the same time make 1½ pints Béchamel sauce flavoured with Parmesan, salt, pepper, a bayleaf and plenty of nutmeg.

Preheat the oven to Reg 3½/340°. When everything is ready remove the bayleaf from the sauce. Put a layer of meat in a buttered gratin dish, add a layer of Béchamel, then a layer of slightly overlapping pieces of lasagne. Add more meat, more Béchamel, more lasagne and finish with a layer of meat covered with Béchamel. Sprinkle the top with cheese, dot with butter and bake for ¾ hour.

☐ *This is not worth making for less than six, but is well worth doing for more.*

For 6

Basic Savoury Pancakes (1)

Savoury Pancakes (2)

4 oz plain flour
1 egg
½ pint milk
salt

Beat the egg thoroughly into the milk. Season the flour and stir in the milk and egg mixture gradually, to make a smooth lump-free batter.

Beat for several minutes with a wooden spoon with the bowl of the spoon turned over, so that the air in the hollow of the spoon gets into the batter, or beat with a balloon whisk or an electric beater. Allow to stand for two hours before using.

☐ *This mixture makes 6-8 pancakes; make it two hours before it is needed.*

For method of making pancakes see page 200.

Use the same recipe as before but add two teaspoons of melted butter to the mixture, after you have combined the other ingredients. This makes the pancakes just slightly richer, and they can be put under the grill without drying up.

Layered Pancakes

8 pancakes (page 53)

Use two kinds of filling. Choose from spinach, chicken, fish, or diced hard-boiled egg and bacon. Alternate the layers, stacking the pancakes up, one on top of another, in a deep dish with the fillings in between. Cover with a final layer of sauce, cheese is the best for this, and put in a moderate oven to heat through. It is best to use hot sauces and pancakes to cut down the time in the oven as much as possible. Serve cut in slices like a cake.

For 4

Chicken Pancakes

12 large pancakes (page 53)
4 oz button mushrooms
1 oz flour
1 oz butter
½ pint chicken stock, or failing this, milk
salt and freshly ground pepper
½–¾ lb cooked left-over chicken, chopped or pulled
    into manageable pieces
parsley, chopped
Emmenthal cheese, freshly grated, or ½ pint cheese
    sauce
butter

Make the pancakes and keep hot. Peel the mushrooms and simmer the peel in the chicken stock. Strain the stock and add the sliced mushrooms, simmer a few minutes more.

Make a white roux of the flour and butter and add the stock and mushrooms gradually. Season and let the sauce cook slowly for ten minutes. Add the chicken pieces together with any jelly that has set in their dish. Stir in the chopped parsley; season again if necessary. Put a line of the filling into each pancake, and fold in or roll up with the ends open. Lay the pancakes side by side in a gratin dish, and either sprinkle with cheese and melted butter and cook under a slow grill for 15–20 minutes or until hot through, or pour the cheese sauce over and then brown — this prevents them from drying up.

For 6

Fish Pancakes

8 large pancakes
1 oz butter
1 oz flour
½ pint milk, or fish stock if you have it
½ lb cold cooked fish such as cod or haddock (fresh
    or smoked), salmon etc.
2 oz Parmesan, freshly grated
salt and freshly ground pepper
thin cream, or top of the milk

Make the pancakes and keep them hot. Make a
sauce with the butter, flour and milk, or milk and fish
stock. Add the cheese, salt and pepper. Use half the
sauce to bind the fish, which must be skinned, boned
and flaked. Check the seasoning. Put a line of the
fish mixture down the edge of each pancake, roll
them up and lay them in a flameproof dish. Pour on
the rest of the sauce, with a little cream or top of the
milk if available, and grill gently until warmed
through and lightly browned.

For 4

Spinach Pancakes

These are made like fish pancakes (this page) but
with spinach, cooked, drained and chopped, instead
of the fish, added to the sauce. You can use frozen
spinach but add some grated cheese to the sauce for
flavour.

Gnocchi with Potatoes and Pâte à Choux

1 lb potatoes, boiled and sieved dry, with salt and a
   pinch of nutmeg
½ pint water (or just under)
1½ oz butter, cut in pieces
2 oz flour
salt and freshly ground pepper
2 eggs
3 oz Parmesan, grated
¾ pint cheese sauce

Put the water and butter in a pan, bring it to the boil, draw aside and instantly tip in the seasoned flour, beating until the mixture is smooth and leaves the sides of the pan. Beat the eggs lightly and add gradually to the warm mixture, beating all the time. Mix this pâte à choux with the sieved, dryish potatoes and half the Parmesan cheese. Make little rolls of about one dessertspoon of the mixture on a floured board. Put a wide shallow pan of salted water on to simmer — boiling will break up the gnocchi. Drop them into the water one at a time. Do only a few at once to allow for their increasing size. When they are done (after about 10 minutes) they will float to the top. Remove them with a perforated spoon and let them drain on a folded cloth, until they are cool. Make a rich cheese sauce. Butter a gratin dish and lay the gnocchi in it without overlapping. Pour over the sauce, sprinkle with the rest of the Parmesan and put under a medium grill to heat through and brown.

□ *A laborious recipe but the result is delicate and luxurious.*

For 6 as a first course, or 4 as a main dish

Gnocchi with Semolina

½ pint milk
½ pint water
1 onion
bayleaf
5 tablespoons semolina
salt and freshly ground pepper
½ oz butter
3 oz Parmesan, grated
tomato sauce (page 185)

Infuse the milk and water with the sliced onion, bayleaf and salt, simmering very gently for five minutes. Strain and return to the pan. Bring back to the boil and add the semolina, beating with a wooden spoon until smooth. Cook for ten minutes over a moderate heat, stirring often to prevent lumps. Remove from the heat and add 2 oz grated Parmesan, the butter and freshly ground black pepper. Beat thoroughly, then spread the mixture evenly in a flat oiled dish. Cool, and you will find it has set enough to cut in one-inch squares or rounds. Arrange the gnocchi overlapping on a buttered gratin dish, sprinkle with the remaining Parmesan, dot with butter and put under a hot grill. When brown serve with tomato sauce and more cheese.

□ *Of all gnocchi these are probably the easiest to make at home. They are quite light and have a marvellous flavour.*

For 4

Green Gnocchi

1 lb spinach, washed and chopped
¾ lb Ricotta cheese or cottage cheese, sieved
2 egg yolks
4 tablespoons Parmesan, grated
½ teaspoon salt
1–2 oz flour
melted butter for serving

Cook the spinach (if using fresh spinach) in a little salted water for five minutes. If using frozen spinach allow it to thaw completely. In both cases drain very well so that the spinach is dry. You can purée the spinach at this point for a finer texture. Mix thoroughly with the Ricotta, egg yolks, half the Parmesan and the salt. Shape into little balls the size of a large marble, rolling them lightly in flour. You can prepare them in advance to this point — they will keep for several hours in a cool place. Then drop them one by one into a large pan of simmering salted water, where they will rise to the surface. After four minutes' gentle simmering, remove them carefully with a perforated spoon. Put in a hot serving dish and serve sprinkled with melted butter and the rest of the Parmesan. They are feathery light, pale green melting globes, a marvellous light lunch or start to a dinner-party.

For 4

Parsley Dumplings

4 oz plain flour
2 level teaspoons baking powder
½ teaspoon salt
1 oz butter
1 egg
handful of chopped parsley
milk

Mix the flour, salt and baking powder. Cut the butter into small pieces and rub it into the flour. Mix the egg and parsley and stir into the flour mixture. Add milk little by little to make a stiff dough. Form into little balls the size of marbles. Drop them on to the top of your stew, which is already cooking, about 20 minutes before you want to eat. Put the lid on and leave for 20 minutes; they will be twice the size and very light.

☐ *Delicious with stews or casseroles of beef or game, as an alternative to potatoes.*

For 6

Pizza

¾ pint well-seasoned tomato sauce made with
   tinned or fresh tomatoes (page 185)
1 or 2 Mozzarella cheeses or ¼–½ lb Bel Paese
anchovy fillets
black olives, stoned
oregano, basil or marjoram
olive oil
1 lb pizza dough (opposite)

Preheat oven to Reg 6/400°. When the dough has
risen and been kneaded, shape it into flat rounds or
oblongs the size of the pizza you want to make, and
lay them in greased tins. Spread liberally with the
tomato sauce and lay slices of cheese, anchovy
fillets and black olives on top. Sprinkle with oregano,
basil or marjoram and a generous amount of olive
oil, about 1 dessertspoon for each small pizza.
Don't take the filling right to the edges, although it
is tempting, because the crust makes a sort of bank
to keep the filling in while it cooks. Leave 20 minutes
to rise again. Bake at Reg 6/400° for 15 minutes,
then at Reg 5/375° for a further 15–20 minutes.
This is a Neapolitan pizza. There are lots of other
fillings you can put in a basic pizza, but perhaps
the simple olive and anchovy is really the best of all.

3 large or 6 small

Other variations

American Hot: slices of red pepper sautéed in oil,
slices of hot Italian sausage and strips of fresh or
bottled chillies on top of the usual tomato and
cheese.

Mushroom: mushrooms sliced and lightly sautéed in
oil or butter, instead of anchovies and olives.

American Sweet: slices of red pepper sautéed in oil
and slices of ordinary salami or sausage, marjoram
and the usual tomato and cheese.

Onion: the Neapolitan pizza with lightly fried onion
rings strewn on with the anchovies etc.

Aglio e Olio: simply garlic, olive oil and fresh chopped
marjoram — no cheese, no tomatoes.

Alla Romana: without tomatoes or anchovies but
with sliced Mozzarella, Parmesan and fresh basil.

Mussels: with tomato sauce, oregano, garlic, parsley
and little shelled mussels (or clams).

The pizza can also be covered with another piece of
dough before baking if full of extra juicy filling,
although this can make it stodgy.

Pizza Dough

1 lb flour
1 oz yeast (or ½ oz freshly bought dried yeast)
1½ teaspoons salt
¼–½ pint water
3 tablespoons olive oil

Dissolve the salt in ½ pint warm water (blood heat or less). Put the flour in a bowl, make a well in the centre and pour in the yeast, dissolved in about two tablespoons of the warm water. Mix with one hand, gradually adding more water with the other. When you have a stringy mass give it a few good turns and nudges, and when it is the right consistency — elastic, springy and not wet — put it in a lump in a large bowl, cover with a floured cloth and a lid and leave it to rise for an hour or so, until it has about doubled in size. Take it out, knead it well, then add the oil, working in a small quantity at a time with your hands. When it has absorbed about three tablespoons and is a good pliable, smooth consistency again, make it into three or four nice flat rounds and leave them to prove for 20 minutes. Then put on the sauce, cheese etc. Alternatively put the sauce and cheese on before proving. In the *Pizza Express* they don't prove before baking, so if you are in a hurry you can leave out this step, but the pizza may not be so light.

☐ *You can also buy dough from bakers who bake their own bread.*

For 4 pizzas

Norfolk Dumplings

8 oz self-raising flour
1 teaspoon salt
water

Sift the flour and salt into a bowl and mix with water to make a dough. Shape the dough into balls the size of a walnut. A good way of doing this is in the floured palm of your hand. Put in a steamer and steam exactly 20 minutes. Do not remove the lid during cooking time or the dumplings will spoil, and remember that dumplings are like soufflés: they will not wait. Called fillers these are served with gravy or butter or brown sugar. Called swimmers they are served with jam or syrup. You can steam these dumplings by sitting them on the top of a dryish stew for 20 minutes, keeping the pot closed. They are very good, too, with chopped herbs in them, parsley or marjoram.

For 4 or more

Simple Fritter Batter

4 oz flour
1 egg
salt
1 tablespoon oil
¼ pint milk, or less

Sieve the flour with a pinch of salt into a bowl, and make a well in the centre. Separate the egg and keep the white aside. Mix the yolk carefully with the flour, blending well with a wooden spoon. Add the oil and then the milk, a little at a time, drawing in the flour gradually. When you have a thick, smooth, creamy batter stop adding milk and beat the mixture well. Allow it to stand as long as possible in a cool place; about two hours is ideal. Just before you need it, beat the white of the egg stiffly and fold it into the batter.
This is for fritters to be fried in deep oil. If using it for sweet things you can add a spoonful of liqueur to replace some of the milk.

☐ *This is good for sweet fritters, or fairly solid things like corned-beef fritters.*

Enough for fritters for 4–6 people

Delicate Fritter Batter

4 oz flour
3 tablespoons melted butter
¼ pint lukewarm water
salt
1 egg white

About two hours before it is needed, start the batter. In a bowl mix the flour, a pinch of salt and the melted butter, then add water gradually until you have a thickish creamy mixture. Let it stand in a cool place. At the last moment beat the egg white to soft peaks and fold it into the batter mixture.

☐ *Very good for savoury fritters, vegetables etc.*

Enough for fritters for 4–6 people

FISH

Fish

Fishmongers seem to be a vanishing race, and if you live inland and can find a fish that has been for a swim in the last week, you are lucky. If you do have an excellent fishmonger, or live near the sea and know that the catch has just come in, fish is one of the greatest treats. But it is an absolute must to have fish that is fresh; you can tell by the smell, and by the general glossiness of its condition. Most books recommend a look at the gills to see how fresh a fish is, but few fishmongers are very agreeable about this; and beware, Tante Marie advises, of those who brighten the gills with lamb's blood just to deceive you (as if they would bother . Anyway fresh fish looks fresh and not at all dingy, and if it is a herring it will be floppy and slippery, if a mackerel stiff and a radiant blue or green. You should always ask the man behind the counter what he recommends. If he wants you to come back he is unlikely to suggest something doubtful.

Shellfish have sadly become more and more expensive, but fresh cockles and mussels really are worth buying (or looking for by the seaside, *always* checking first that the source is pure). It is no longer so easy to catch your own shrimps, but the small brown British ones, if you can get them, are worth having; although they are fiddly to shell, they have a really good flavour and are lovely for tea with brown bread and butter. Fish from the freezer is second best, for although it is spanking fresh when it goes into the freezing plant, most of it comes out in such unpromising looking doorsteps that it makes dreary material for any recipe.

Besides, it is cheaper to make your own fish fingers and fishcakes, though perhaps a bore, and it is much more pleasurable to buy cod cutlets from a real cod, with luminous golden green freckled skin and actual bones — inconvenience food if you like, but worth it.

The prices of fish whizz up and down with the seasons and weather, but roughly speaking mackerel are best in summer and cheap all the year round, herrings are good all the year round; smoked haddock are less good in spring and early summer, but often more worth buying than a lot of other fish.

Make sure you get undyed haddock on the bone. If it is dyed bright yellow and filleted, you are possibly buying smoked cod, which is cheaper but has a much stronger flavour and is often more salty, which makes it a less useful fish for cooking. Sprats are best in winter and bloaters and kippers (again look for undyed fish) in summer. Cod is expensive in the spring.

This book doesn't mention salmon, turbot, halibut, lobster and so on because they are practically the most expensive food you can buy, unless you have a fisherman in the family. Lots of people have, but even so fish is generally a neglected form of food — partly, one suspects, because it makes the house smell when it is cooking. If you bake it in the oven, covered with foil, this is not much of a problem. Old-fashioned cooks often baked it in a covered buttered tin with no liquid, and it does stay very succulent cooked like this; it is also worth buying a second-hand fish kettle for the occasions when you want to steam a whole cod or haddock (or salmon-trout if you are in luck) because it makes the operation of getting the fish out of the pan, in one piece, a great deal less tricky. It comes in quite useful, too, for sterilising bottles. About the most useless piece of equipment you could find is a fish-shaped frying pan; because it is so badly balanced it tips over constantly, and it holds no more than an ordinary round pan. A fish-scaler could be useful if you were constantly tearing huge scales off gigantic fish, but this is easily done with a knife, held rather flat against the skin and scraped lightly from tail to head in short strokes.

If you are poaching fish (which is quite different from boiling it) it is the easiest thing to make a delicate *court-bouillon*. Put in a large pan one part wine vinegar to ten parts water, with plenty of salt, peppercorns, sprigs of parsley and finely sliced onions and carrots, and boil everything for twenty minutes to half an hour before you add the fish. You can also make a quick stock with the heads, bones and trimmings of the fish simmered in water with onion, parsley, salt and peppercorns, to which you add a dash of white wine if you can. Three of the best things to serve with plain poached fish are the herb butters (page 186), Hollandaise sauce (page 179), and a Béchamel (page 178) made partly with the fish stock and coloured brilliant green with handfuls of fresh chopped parsley.

Fresh Cod with Aïoli

2–3 lbs centre cut of cod (must be fresh)
12 egg-sized potatoes, preferably new, washed but
   not peeled
6 hard-boiled eggs, 1 lb cleaned carrots
6 courgettes   } if in season, but fish,
1 lb French beans   } carrots, potatoes and eggs
6 small green artichokes } form a very good dish
                   } together
aïoli (page 176) *or* melted butter
court-bouillon:
2 quarts water, ½ pint cider vinegar
1 sliced onion, 1 stick celery, 1 bayleaf, 12 peppercorns

Boil the ingredients for the court-bouillon together
for 25 minutes and allow to cool to blood heat. Add
two teaspoons of salt. Cook the cod in this by simmering for ten minutes to a pound. Boil or steam the
potatoes and other vegetables separately, until just
done (avoid overdoing them).

Serve everything on a large dish, each kind of
vegetable and the eggs in separate groups, the fish
in the centre. Serve with plenty of stinging strong
aïoli (or melted butter for those who don't like
garlic).

☐ *An English version of salt cod with aïoli, it makes
a marvellous weekend lunch, and is very good for a
large family.*

For 4–6

Cod with Cheese Sauce

1 cod cutlet per person
1 pint court-bouillon (this page)
½ pint cheese sauce (page 36)
butter
2 tablespoons cheese, grated

Poach the cod steaks gently in the court-bouillon
for 15–20 minutes, while you make the cheese sauce.
Put half the well-seasoned sauce in the bottom of a
gratin dish, then the drained, poached fish. Pour
the rest of the sauce over the top, dot with butter,
sprinkle with grated cheese and bake in a moderate
oven until browned, or put under a gentle grill.

For 2

Cod Mayonnaise with Capers

1 whole fresh cod weighing about 6 lbs, or 3½ lbs
   centre cut of cod
court-bouillon (page 64)
½ pint mayonnaise (page 180) made with the caper
   vinegar
capers

Buy the whole fresh cod on the bone, remove the
head and cook this in the court-bouillon in a huge
pan or fish kettle for 20 minutes. Allow the court-
bouillon to cool to blood-heat, take out the cod's
head and put in the rest of the fish. Poach it gently
with the lid on for 10 minutes per lb. When just
cooked, but not falling to pieces, take out the fish
and drain it. Remove the skin and flake the flesh
from the bones.
Make the mayonnaise with a little caper vinegar
and a little wine or cider vinegar, and thin it down
with wine vinegar until it is the consistency of
thick cream, *or* use cream or water; add a handful
of capers. Pile the cod flakes on a dish, pour the
mayonnaise over and chill. Dot the mayonnaise
with a few more capers.

For 8–10

Cod Portugaise

4 cod cutlets
3 tablespoons lemon juice
4 tablespoons olive oil
12 peppercorns
salt
1 bayleaf
1 clove garlic, crushed
½ pint pizzaiola sauce (page 182)
parsley

Make a marinade from the lemon juice, olive oil,
peppercorns, salt, bayleaf and crushed clove of
garlic. Marinate the fish in this for not less than
half an hour, turning once. Drain the cutlets,
put them in a buttered oven dish and bake, covered,
for half an hour at Reg 4/350°. Heat the pizzaiola
sauce, pour some over each piece of fish and return
to the oven for ten minutes. Serve sprinkled with
freshly chopped parsley.

For 4

Filleted Herrings in Oatmeal

2 good herrings
handful porridge oats
salt and freshly ground pepper
lard
1 lemon or fresh tomato sauce (page 185)

Mix the oats with salt and pepper on a board or
plate and pat them onto the opened, filleted fish.
Fry in lard, top first so they end up skin side down.
They take about 2½ minutes each side, depending
on the size of the fish. Serve with lemon wedges or
with fresh tomato sauce.

For 2

Stuffed Herrings

4 herrings
4 oz fresh breadcrumbs
1 oz butter, well softened
chopped parsley, savory or tarragon
lemon rind, grated
egg to bind
salt and freshly ground pepper

Remove the scales from the fish (1). Cut off the
fishes' heads, removing the innards at the same
time by leaving them attached to the head (2).
With a very sharp knife, cut the fish open along
the backbone, ending at the tail (3). Smooth your
finger along one side of the bone, and the fish falls
in half like a book falling open.
Hold the tail in one hand, slip the knife under the
tail end of the bone to start it off, and pull (4).
The backbone comes out like a zip, all in one piece
(5), if the fish are not frozen stiff. Pick out the
remaining bones (6).
Mix all except the herrings together and season well.
Open the herrings, remove the backbones, put the
stuffing inside, press together lightly and bake in
a moderately low oven, Reg 3/325°, for half an
hour.

☐ *A lot of people object to eating herrings because of
all the spiky little bones that seem to get in every
mouthful. It is very easy to take the bones out and you
are left with a very good fish.*

For 4

1

2

3

4

5

6

Marinated Mackerel with Marjoram

6 mackerel
3 bayleaves
glass white wine or cider
¼–½ pint cider vinegar or wine vinegar
¼–½ pint water
sprigs of marjoram, or failing this oregano or parsley
12 peppercorns
salt

Mackerel Stuffed with Gooseberries

1 mackerel per person
1 or 2 oz gooseberries per mackerel
salt and freshly ground pepper
sugar

Get the fishmonger to fillet the mackerel, or do it yourself (see page 66). Cut the fillets in two lengthwise. Roll the fillets up from the tail end and put in a fireproof dish all facing the same way and with all the silver to one side and the dark blue to the other. Pour over the wine and vinegar. Add enough water to cover. Put in the marjoram and peppercorns and a little salt and cook in a very slow oven, Reg 2/300°, for one hour. Allow to cool, when they will set in a nicely-flavoured jelly.

☐ *You can also do this with herrings.*

For 6

Simmer the gooseberries in a little water, mashing while they cook, until you have a purée. Season generously with salt, pepper and sugar.
Fillet the fish (see page 66) leaving them joined along the belly. Open them flat and spread the purée on one side. Press the fish together again, lay in a buttered dish and cover with greased paper, or wrap them individually in foil parcels. Bake in a moderate oven, Reg 4/350°, for 30 minutes or longer. depending on the size of the fish.

Kipper Salad

2 good uncooked kippers — these must be fresh,
   undyed, old-fashioned kippers, not frozen or
   wrapped
oil
1 lemon
1 small onion, sliced thinly into rings
1 large cold cooked potato, peeled and diced
1 green pepper (optional), seeded and diced
salt, freshly ground pepper and a pinch of paprika
parsley, chopped

Skin and bone the uncooked kippers; this is quite
easy if they are fresh and juicy. Cut them into small
squares, and cover with oil and the juice of half the
lemon while you prepare the other ingredients. Put
a dressing of oil and lemon, salt and pepper on the
potatoes. Mix the onion and green pepper with the
kipper. Serve the kipper salad sprinkled with
parsley and the potato salad sprinkled with paprika,
side by side.

For 2

Seviche

1 lb sea-bass or other firm-fleshed fish, boned and
   cut into half-inch cubes
1 onion, chopped
1 small green pimento, finely chopped
juice of 2 lemons (or limes if you can get them)
1 small green chilli, finely chopped
1 tablespoon olive oil
handful of fresh parsley, finely chopped
salt

Mix all the ingredients together well and put them
in a covered bowl in the refrigerator overnight.
That's it; eat it raw. It is 'cooked' by the action of
the lemon or lime juice, but the trick is not to
mention this until after people have eaten it. The
fish must be very fresh.

□ *A Latin-American dish.*

For 6

Kedgeree 1

1 ½ lbs smoked haddock on the bone
½ pint milk
½ pint water
12 oz rice
2 oz flour
1 ½ oz butter
2 tablespoons cheese, grated, *or* ½ teaspoon curry
   powder
3 hard-boiled eggs

Poach the haddock gently in milk and water until
the flesh comes off the bones easily (after about ten
minutes). Keep aside the liquid in which it is cooked.
Wash the rice and boil in plenty of salted water for
12 minutes; drain and wash it well. Make a sauce
with the flour, butter and haddock liquid. If you
like a slight curry flavour, cook the powder in the
butter for a few moments before adding the flour.
If you prefer cheese, leave out the curry and add the
cheese to the sauce. It should be fairly thick, but
the rice will absorb some of it, so if you like sloshy
kedgeree, make the sauce thinner by adding more
milk.
Add the flaked fish, chopped hard-boiled eggs and
cooked, drained rice. Put the mixture in the top of a
double saucepan and steam for 20–30 minutes.
Serve with a lump of butter on each helping.

For 4–6

Kedgeree 2

½ lb cooked smoked haddock
6 oz cooked rice
3 hard-boiled eggs, chopped or sliced
handful cooked peas *or* chopped parsley
butter
salt or freshly ground pepper
2 tablespoons cream

Combine these ingredients in the top of a double
boiler, adding the chopped hard-boiled eggs last of
all, and stir very gently a couple of times while you
heat it through.

☐ *A very good breakfast dish. This is a dryish
kedgeree, but the moisture in the rice and the fish, and
plenty of butter or a couple of tablespoons of cream,
give it a good succulent consistency.*

For 4

Creamed Smoked Haddock

1 lb smoked haddock on the bone
½ pint milk
1 oz butter
¾ oz flour
2 tablespoons Parmesan, grated (optional)
plenty of freshly ground pepper
salt if necessary

Poach the haddock in the milk until it comes easily off the bone — about ten minutes, taking care not to let it burn at the bottom, and then strain the milk into a jug. Remove the skin and bones, and shred the fish as finely as possible with a knife and fork, or sieve through the coarse disc of the mouli, or liquidise for a few seconds.

Make a sauce with the butter, flour and the milk in which the fish was cooked. Add the cheese, pepper and the fish. Taste for salt.

Serve the purée on golden fried bread cut in triangles.

□ *Good for a first course or for supper with a poached egg on top.*

For 2

Fish Pie

¾ lb smoked haddock
¾ lb fresh haddock
1½ lbs potatoes, boiled and mashed with plenty of
    butter and milk
½ oz butter
1½ oz flour
¾ pint milk
½ pint water
1 teaspoon white wine- or cider-vinegar
salt and freshly ground pepper
3 hard-boiled eggs
parsley, chopped

Preheat the oven to Reg 5/375°. Poach the fish in the milk and water for 15 minutes, or until the skin and bones come away easily, basting with the liquid a couple of times. Make a sauce with the butter, flour and enough of the fish liquid to give it the consistency of double cream. Add the vinegar, seasoning, flaked fish, sliced eggs and parsley to the sauce. Arrange the mixture in a pie dish and cover with mashed potato. Dot with butter and bake at Reg 5/375°, for half an hour or until brown. This pie is very much liked by children; if it is for adults you can add chopped scallops sautéed in butter, for the brief glorious couple of months they are in season, but it is excellent anyway.

For 6

Fish Cakes

1½ lbs cod, hake or fresh haddock
4–5 large potatoes, baked and mashed dry
1–2 hard-boiled eggs
for the sauce:
1½ oz butter, 1½ oz flour
¾ pint milk infused with 1 carrot, 1 onion and some
    parsley for 30 minutes
salt and freshly ground pepper
for coating and deep-frying:
1 beaten egg
dried breadcrumbs
lard, oil or dripping

Bake the potatoes, or boil them in their skins.
When cooked, skin and mash them. Cook the fish in
a covered greased dish in a medium oven, Reg 4/350°,
until the bones and skin come away easily. Remove
the skin and bones, flake the fish. Make a stiffish
sauce with the butter, flour and flavoured milk,
plus any liquid given out by the fish while it cooked.
Mix the potato, fish, chopped hard-boiled eggs and
sauce. Season and leave to cool, preferably overnight. When cold make small, round flat cakes or
cork shapes; roll them in flour and pat smooth.
Dip into beaten egg, then breadcrumbs, and fry
three or four minutes in hot deep fat. Drain on
kitchen paper and keep warm until ready to serve.

☐ *Makes 20–24. These are a bore to make and should
be done the day before, but they are far better than any
you can buy.*

For 8–10

Fish Soup (Bouillabaisse)

2 lbs mixed fish. Choose from haddock ; whiting ;
    mullet, red or grey ; brill ; gurnet ; bream ; and
    shellfish as available — mussels ; prawns ;
    scallops etc.
2 onions, 3 cloves garlic, 1 bayleaf
large sprigs thyme, parsley, and fennel (use bulb
    fennel or seeds if no fresh)
2 tomatoes, 1 strip orange peel
large pinch saffron, salt and pepper
4 tablespoons olive oil, dash of white wine
Parmesan, grated, rouille (page 183)
4 slices of French bread dried slowly in the oven

Cut the cleaned fish, scraped to remove the scales,
in two-inch pieces. Make a stock with the bones,
trimmings and heads while you crush the garlic,
and peel and chop the onions and tomatoes.
Put the vegetables in a pan with the garlic, herbs,
orange peel, seasoning, saffron and oil. Cook for
five minutes without browning. Put the coarser
varieties of fish in with the vegetables and strain the
boiling stock over them. They should be covered,
so add water if necessary and a dash of white wine.
Boil fast for five minutes, add the more delicate fish
and boil on for another five to ten minutes. Add the
shellfish five minutes before the end. Remove from
the stove and serve with the toasted bread and a
good stinging rouille (page 183) and grated Parmesan
cheese.

For 4

Squid Risotto

2 lbs squid
1 small onion, sliced
1 clove garlic, sliced
olive oil
1 wineglass red wine
1 glass warm water
1 small tin tomato purée
salt and freshly ground pepper
10 oz Italian rice

Peel the skin from the body of the squid, pull off
the head and with it come the entrails. Take out the
bone from the body and cut the tentacles from the
head; throw away head, bone and innards. Slice the
body into thin rings, chop up the tentacles, and
wash well to get rid of any sand.

Fry the onion and garlic in oil in a sauté pan with a
lid; add the pieces of well-washed squid. Let it
stiffen and become less transparent; add the wine,
let it simmer for five minutes and add salt, pepper
and the tomato purée, plus a glass of warm water.
Cover the pan, turn the heat right down and simmer
for one hour. Add the rice, well washed under
running water, stir from time to time and cook until
tender, 20–30 minutes, adding more warm water if
it becomes dry. Correct the seasoning and serve.

For 4

Deep-fried Sprats

1 lb sprats
deep-frying oil (use a whole bottle, strain it after
    each time you use it and keep it for fish)
seasoned flour
1 lemon

Wash the sprats and pat them dry in a piece of
kitchen paper. Flip each one in a heap of seasoned
flour, shaking off the surplus before dropping them
one by one into hot oil, with a blue haze (*not* smoke)
rising; when pale gold they are done. Drain off the
oil as you take them out and keep the fish hot on a
paper-lined dish in a low oven.

Remove the paper, and serve them, complete with
heads and tails, with lemon wedges. If you haven't
had sprats before they will be a great discovery; they
are simply delicious fried like this. If you are finicky
about bones you can split the sprats before flouring
and remove the backbones, leaving heads and tails
on; they will fry a fraction faster.

For 4

To Prepare and Dress a Crab

Bang the underneath of the back end of the cooked crab on the side of a table, holding the crab by the shell. The body and legs should come away and you can detach this piece. If the crab is watery when you open it up, this does not mean anything is wrong with it.

First scoop out all the soft creamy parts from the inside of the shell. The fresher the crab, the moister and more succulent this part will be. Pile it on a plate. Now from the inside of the body part, in a sort of V, scoop out the brown meat and slush, having first removed the finger-like gills which lie on either side of the V. They are not — and do not even look — edible. Put the brown meat with the creamy meat. Now pull the claws off the body and put them on one side. With a sharp knife make a V-shaped cut, right through the bony body, with the point of the V at the back end so that it falls in three pieces (see diagram). With a skewer, empty all the cavities you have revealed by your cuts, and pile the meat on a separate plate. Crack the claws with a hammer or nutcrackers and pick all the meat out, again with the help of a skewer. Add to the other white meat. Add some dried, browned breadcrumbs and a little salt and pepper to the brown meat, and mash it with a fork. It gives a good texture and makes it go further. Flake all the white meat. Put the two kinds of meat in separate piles on the same dish, and serve either with mayonnaise, or simply with lemon juice or even vinegar, and brown bread and butter.

A crab five inches across the shell will serve two people with ease. It is very filling and incredibly cheap compared with most other shellfish, and it's certainly just as good. Some people put chopped hard-boiled egg white in the white meat to make it go further.

It is worth dressing your own crab because it soon dries up and loses its flavour once it has been done. It is perhaps a bit cheaper too, as you know exactly what proportion of crab to breadcrumbs you are getting, the sort of information no fishmonger would think of revealing!

Hot Crab

8 oz crabmeat (the meat from a 1 lb crab)
½ pint thickish Béchamel sauce made from 1 oz
    flour, 1 oz butter and ½ pint milk
½ teaspoon made mustard
1 tablespoon chopped parsley
1 tablespoon lemon juice or white wine
1 tablespoon cream
salt and freshly ground pepper

Flake the crabmeat, add to the Béchamel with the
mustard, parsley, lemon juice or wine, cream and
seasoning. Use the hot mixture to fill little pastry
shells or serve it on triangles of bread, fried golden
brown in a mixture of oil and butter.

□ *This is only good with really fresh crab.*

For 2

Winkles and Cockles

Gather the winkles from a part of the beach that is
known to be clean and pure. Try to take some clean
sea water home, to cook them in. Wash them well
under a running tap, scrambling them round with
your hand, to remove all the mud and sand.

Put a pan of well-salted water or sea water, deep
enough to cover the winkles, on to boil. When the
water comes to the boil throw them in and turn the
heat up. When it returns to a full boil, let them
cook for one or two minutes, then drain and run
under the cold tap to cool.

Eat them with a pin or toothpick, removing their
little black lids before you dexterously hook them
out. Some people put vinegar on, but it is not an
improvement. They are very good for tea with
bread and butter.

Wash cockles well, as for winkles. Bring some *well-
salted* water to the boil. Throw in the cockles, turn
the heat to moderate and watch carefully. As soon
as they open take them out. Very good with drinks
taken out of their shells, and with a squeeze of
lemon and a sprinkling of parsley.

Fried Cockles

2 quarts fresh cockles
2 lemons
masses of freshly ground black pepper
a little salt
olive oil for frying

Wash and dry the cockles very thoroughly.
Heat two or three tablespoons of oil in a large
frying pan. Drop the cockles in, stir them round
until they open, then smother them in freshly
ground pepper and the juice of two lemons. Hardly
any salt is needed. Eat straight away.

□ *In Spain these are served with drinks.*

For 6–8

Grilled Mussels

1 quart mussels
1–2 oz salted butter
3 cloves garlic, finely chopped
handful fresh parsley, finely chopped

Wash the mussels in cold water to clean off the worst of the mud. Cut off the beards, stray limpets (best banged with the back of a knife) and spots of mud. Wash again in clear cold water. Bring about an inch of water to the boil in a large pan. Throw in the mussels and cook, covered, over a high heat, shaking the pan a couple of times, until they are all opened. It only takes a few minutes. Meanwhile chop the parsley and garlic finely and mash them into the butter with a fork. When the drained opened mussels are cool enough to handle, remove the empty half of each shell and put a hazelnut of garlic butter on each mussel. Put them in a grill pan under a moderate grill until the butter is bubbling hot; serve with plenty of bread to mop up the juice. About 12 mussels each is plenty. They are rather like juicy snails.

For 2

Cockle and Mussel Risotto

2 quarts cockles and mussels (1 quart of each)
2 tablespoons olive oil
1 medium onion, chopped
8 oz Italian rice
½ glass white wine
1 large pinch saffron
1 red pimento, chopped

As you are going to use the liquid from the shell-fish to cook the rice, it is very important to wash them thoroughly. Since they are full of salty water, do not add any more salt to the water in which you cook them.

Take a large pan with a lid. Bring to the boil sufficient water to come half way up the cockles and mussels. Throw them in, put on the lid and shake the pan once or twice. After five minutes they should all be opened; strain off the liquid and remove most of the shells. Keep the shellfish warm in their liquid while you cook the rice.

Heat the olive oil in a wide shallow pan and cook the chopped onion in it for about 10 minutes without browning; add the rice and stir it round until it becomes transparent.

Dissolve the saffron in the wine, if using powder, or soak the strands in it, and add to the rice. Stir until the rice has absorbed most of the wine. Taste the shellfish liquid and if it is too salt dilute it with fresh water. Pour about half a pint on to the rice, stir it about and add the chopped red pimento. Cover the pan and let the rice simmer, adding more liquid as necessary. When the rice is tender, stir in the shelled cockles and mussels, heat through and pile into a heated dish. Decorate the top in a haphazard way with the cockles and mussels left in their shells.

☐ *This can be made with either cockles or mussels or with both.*

For 4

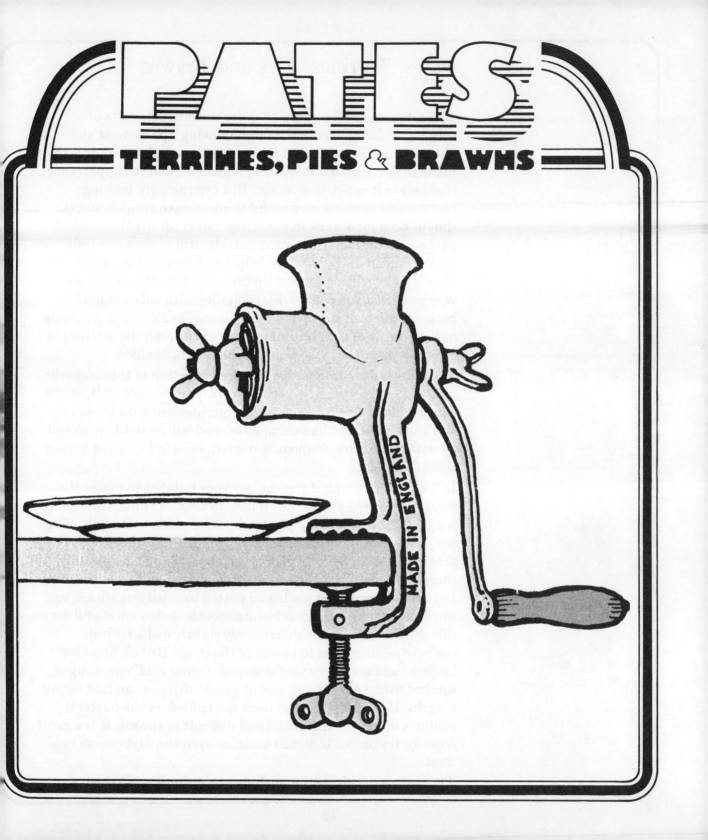

PATES

TERRINES, PIES & BRAWHS

Pâtés, Terrines, Pies and Brawns

Pâtés, terrines and pies are all quite considerable tests of cooking ability, because although mincing up the meat and putting the thing together is all quite straightforward, it is the blend of flavours that demands judgement, and the appearance that makes it appetising or not. But even an ugly-looking home-made pâté is a very useful thing to have around, and it should keep for a week in the refrigerator. Ideally the finished pâté should be nicely browned outside, still pink inside (salt pork included in the mixture helps) and enclosed in a good clear layer of jelly or some crisp brown pastry. When you are very practised you can marble each slice with cubes of pork back fat, fillets of the meat you are using, and perhaps pistachio nuts or pieces of ham or tongue layered through the mixture in carefully placed lines, so that each slice gets its share.

The meat is flavoured with a balanced selection of thyme, garlic, juniper berries, bay, mace, lemon-peel, peppercorns, salt, white wine and brandy. Once you have experimented with these you will know what you like using most, and will be unlikely to end up with what is too frequently offered, even in France, a boring sort of meat-loaf.

It is a great triumph if you can get your butcher to mince the meat for you every time, but if not, an electric automatic chopper is a great help in making pâté and potted meat, as it really chops the meat instead of squeezing and grinding it. Otherwise it is the mincer and plenty of energy, and apart from this the only equipment necessary is a terrine or bowl that will go in the oven. Potted meats are best made and potted in small quantities, so small, straight-sided, round white cocotte dishes are useful for this. Potted meat and fish have very rightly had a revival recently — they used to be one of the staple British breakfast foods — and are a very useful way of storing cold ham, tongue, smoked fish or almost any sort of game until you can face eating it again. Don't serve potted meat too chilled, as the butter it contains makes it rather solid and difficult to spread. It is a great treat for tea on hot buttered toast, or even as a first course to a meal.

The recipes in this section include one for pork pie, which is tremendously fiddly to do, so don't be surprised if the first one you make looks a bit strange; it gets better with practice, and it is a lovely thing to be able to produce at a picnic. Of course you can perfectly well buy pork pies, but that is about the limit of charcuterie in this country. You can't always buy interesting pâtés and rillettes or brawns, or things set in jelly or specially good salads made with calves' heads, so you just have to make them if you want them. Luckily they nearly all use the cheaper pieces of meat and are inexpensive provided you don't count the cost of your time.

Chicken Liver Pâté

½ lb chicken livers, frozen or fresh
1 small shallot, chopped very finely
1 oz butter
2 sage leaves, chopped very finely, or ½ teaspoon
   thyme leaves
1 small clove garlic, mashed
salt and freshly ground black pepper
dash of port, sherry or brandy, or a little white wine

Sort through the chicken livers, washing and drying thoroughly if in doubt, removing strings and yellow areas. Chop into small pieces and sprinkle with salt and pepper while you fry the shallot in a small saucepan in the butter, without browning. Add the seasoned chicken livers, herbs and garlic, and increase the heat a little, stirring constantly with a wooden spoon or wooden fork (an old salad server is useful for this dish). The livers will crumble as you do this. Keep mashing and add the wine, brandy or other alcohol. When all the livers have become pinkish brown (after about five minutes), remove from the heat and continue mashing until the whole thing is smooth. Put into a little soufflé dish, or individual cocotte dishes and serve well chilled. This pâté improves with keeping, but if it is to be kept for several days, pour melted butter on top.

For 4

Pig's Liver Pâté

12 oz pig's liver
4 oz salt (preferably) or fresh belly of pork
1 onion
1 clove garlic
salt, freshly ground pepper, pinch mixed spice
small glass white wine
small glass water
1 pig's foot, split in half
rosemary, bayleaf, thyme and parsley, tied together
   with a thread
bacon fat

Mince the pig's liver and pork with half the onion. Crush the garlic and add it to the meat with the mixed spice, a generous amount of pepper, and salt only if you are using fresh pork. Put the liver mixture into a large terrine or other mould and press down evenly. Pour in the water and wine which should cover the meat by half an inch. Slice up the carrot and remaining onion, and lay them on top of the pâté with the herbs and pig's trotter. Cover the dish with foil and bake in a bain-marie at Reg 2/300° for three hours. Remove the trotter, herbs and vegetables. When cold pour melted bacon fat over the top to seal it. Eat cold the following day when the jelly will be set.

☐ *A very spicy pâté with a good jelly round it.*

Makes 1 lb pâté, for 8–12 people

Rabbit Pâté

1 lb boned rabbit
½ glass white wine
the rabbit liver
1 clove garlic
6 oz streaky green bacon rashers, cut thin
salt and freshly ground pepper
grated lemon peel
nutmeg
1 teaspoon fresh thyme leaves, or ½ teaspoon dried

Marinate the best parts of the rabbit meat, cut in little fillets, in the wine, while you mince the rest of the meat and the liver as finely as you can. Chop the garlic and the bacon, rinds removed, as finely as possible, keeping three or four rashers on one side. Add the chopped bacon and garlic to the meat and season with salt, pepper, a pinch of grated lemon peel, nutmeg and thyme. Press the mixture into a suitable earthenware dish in layers with the fillets. Press flat and cover with the reserved rashers of bacon. Pour over the wine marinade and cover the dish with buttered foil. Place in a bain-marie and cook in a slow oven, Reg 2/300°, for two to three hours. It is done when the pâté shrinks from the sides of the dish. Press with a weight while it cools and sets. Eat cold. This pâté improves with keeping and will last up to a week in the refrigerator.

For 6

Potted Tongue or Ham

8 oz cooked tongue or ham
8 oz butter (cheapest unsalted), clarified (page 220)
½ level teaspoon mace
freshly ground pepper
salt if necessary

Chop up the meat and put in the liquidiser, with 5 oz melted clarified butter, the mace and pepper. Make a fine purée (if you don't have a liquidiser you can do this by pounding it in a pestle and mortar), taste for salt. Pack it into a pot, pressing well down to eliminate air. Chill for half an hour and when firm smooth the top and cover with melted, clarified butter; what is left will just about do the trick. The potted meat is a beautiful pink and should be put in a neutral coloured pot, white, cream or beige, to look its best, with the yellow butter in a layer over the top.

Makes 1 lb, for 8–12

A Raised Pork Pie weighing 2 lbs.

1 lb lean end of belly of pork, or blade (about three
    parts lean to one part fat)
salt and freshly ground pepper
water, dried sage
½ pint stock made with 1 pig's trotter and the trim-
    mings from the pork
for the pastry:
12 oz plain flour, pinch salt, 4 oz lard
¼ pint water, 1 egg yolk (for glaze)

Trim the meat, mince half of it as finely as you can
and chop the other half into pea-sized pieces; it
takes a long time. Season well, add sage to your
liking and moisten with half a wine glass of water.
Preheat the oven to Reg 8/450°.

To make the pie-crust
Sift the flour with the salt and put to keep warm
in a large bowl. Melt the lard, cut in pieces, in the
water in a small saucepan, and then bring to the
boil; as it boils pour it on to the flour. Mix rapidly
with a wooden spoon until it is smooth. Reserve a
quarter of the pastry for the lid, keeping it warm.
Flatten out the rest as soon as it is cool enough to
handle. When it is about quarter to half an inch
thick, mould it into a pie shape on the bottom of a
large greased jam or storage-jar. Lift it, jar and all,
on to a greased baking tin, wait until the crust is
cool, and gently ease the jar away. It may collapse a
bit, but never mind. You should have a case about
five inches in diameter and two or three inches high.

Fill the case with the meat, pressing it down well;
roll out a lid from the last piece of pastry, and damp
the edges with water before sealing it on very carefully. Press the edges together with your fingers and
decorate them by indenting with the back of a knife
at half-inch intervals or by forking. You can
decorate the pie with pastry trimmings cut into
leaves and flowers. Tie a band of oiled greaseproof
paper round the pie. Paint the top with egg yolk,
and make a round hole in the middle for the steam
to escape and to pour the juice through.

Bake in the centre of a hot oven for half an hour
and then turn the heat down to Reg 5/375° and
cook for another hour. Remove the pie and allow it
to cool a little. Strain the pig's foot stock and reduce
to about ⅓ pint. Season with salt, take it off the
heat and pour it on to half a teaspoon of gelatine in a
jug to make sure it sets. Stir and allow to cool a
little. Fill the pie with this liquid, using a small
funnel. Let it set and keep the pie overnight if
possible. Eat it cold.

For 6–8 people

1

2

3

4

5

6

Cornish Pasties

10 oz steak, well trimmed and cut up very small
1 small potato, peeled and cut up small
1 onion, peeled and chopped finely
parsley, chopped finely
salt and freshly ground pepper
3 tablespoons gravy, stock or water
¾ lb shortcrust pastry made from 8 oz plain flour,
    3½ oz fat, pinch salt and water to bind
1 egg, beaten, or milk, to glaze pastry

Preheat oven to Reg 7/425°. Mix the steak, potato, onion, parsley, salt and pepper, and moisten with the liquid. Roll out the pastry and cut out six circles with the help of a saucer. Put a dollop of the mixture on the centre of each, brush round the edges with beaten egg or milk, and fold the pastry up pinching the edges together in a pretty serpentine pattern. Place on a greased tin, brush with more beaten egg or milk, prick the tops with a fork to let out the steam and bake in the top of the oven for 10–15 minutes to cook the pastry; then turn the oven down to Reg 2/300°, and depending on the quality and tenderness of the steak, bake for a further ½–1 hour. To reheat, put for 15 minutes in a low oven.

6 smallish pasties

84

Brawn

half a pig's head, singed, with the teeth removed,
  split in three pieces by the butcher
2 onions, 4 carrots
2 turnips, 2 leeks
2 sticks celery
bouquet garni
4 or 5 peppercorns, salt
bunch of fresh parsley
1 lemon
2 hard-boiled eggs, sliced
½ bottle of dry white wine or cider

Clean the pig's head with a damp cloth and put it in a pan with the cleaned chopped vegetables, herbs, peppercorns and a little salt. Cover with water and white wine or cider and simmer for three hours, until it is falling apart. Strain off the liquid, skim off the fat and return the liquid to the pan. Add lemon juice and a piece of lemon peel and reduce by half. Taste for seasoning — add a drop more lemon juice if too bland. Meanwhile discard the vegetables, remove the fat and bones from the meat and skin the tongue. Put all the lean meat and tongue on a board and chop it fairly finely. Chop the parsley and mix into the liquid. Put a layer of hard-boiled eggs in the bottom of a basin, put in some of the meat, pour in the liquid. Add the rest of the meat. Put a weighted plate on top of the brawn and leave it to set in the refrigerator for several hours or overnight. Serve with a green salad or as an hors d'oeuvre.

☐ *Suitable also for calf's head.*

For 6–8

Rabbit in Jelly

1 ½ lbs rabbit cut in pieces
1 large onion, sliced
1 pig's foot, split
1 bunch parsley
1 lemon
small glass white wine if available
salt and 6 peppercorns

Put the rabbit pieces in a large pan with the sliced onion, pig's foot, a few sprigs of the parsley, a strip of lemon peel, wine, a little salt and the peppercorns. Just cover with cold water, bring to the boil, skim, and simmer very slowly, covered, for about 1½ hours, until the meat comes off the bones easily. Strain and return the liquid to the pan with the pig's trotter. Put in a fresh piece of lemon peel and simmer, uncovered, until the liquid is reduced to one pint. Skim, and flavour with lemon juice and more salt if necessary. Strain the liquid, skim again and add a good handful of chopped parsley. Put the rabbit meat pulled from the bones and the pink inside pieces of the pig's foot (scarcely visible little scraps of delicious meat) into a square or oblong earthenware dish. Pour the liquid over the meat and chill. It will keep three or four days in the refrigerator. For a very firm jelly dissolve a leaf of gelatine, or half an ounce of powdered gelatine, in the liquid, before you add the parsley. Instead of the parsley you can put half a cucumber, cut into small cubes, into the dish with the meat, but as the cucumber is watery the jelly will not stay firm quite as long.

☐ *Ideal for a cold lunch on a hot summer day.*

For 4–6

Galantine of Breast of Veal

Boning a Breast (Lamb or Veal)

3 lbs breast of veal, boned (keep the bones)
6 oz minced pork, or sausage meat
6 oz ham or tongue, or 3 oz of each
1 small onion, finely chopped, softened in butter
1 small glass white wine
salt, pepper, parsley, thyme
1 oz butter
½ pint stock
2 onions, chopped
2 carrots, chopped
bouquet garni
for prettiness : truffles or pistachio nuts (optional)

Using the veal bones and whatever else you like, make a stock while you prepare the stuffing. Cut the ham or tongue into small pieces, but don't mince. Mix into the minced pork or sausage meat, season well, add herbs, wine, softened onions and truffles or pistachio nuts. Spread the mixture on the boned veal and roll it up. Tie it up with easily seen thread, leaving long ends. Melt the butter in a flameproof casserole, brown the rolled veal all over, remove it and put in the chopped onions, carrots and bouquet garni. Let them sweat for several minutes, then add stock to cover the vegetables, replace the meat, bring the liquid to the boil, cover and continue cooking in the oven at Reg 2/300° for two hours, basting occasionally. When it is ready remove the meat and leave it to cool. Untie it and spoon a little of the cooking liquid over the meat, just before it sets, to give it a shine. You may have to do this basting several times.

☐ *Serve the veal cold in neat slices with salads. This stuffing can also be used to stuff a boned duck or chicken (pages 138–9).*

For at least 10

(1) Breasts are sold sometimes complete, or as shown by the dotted line, halved. The following diagrams deal with the half that has the bones in, left and right sides.

(2) With a sharp knife (A), cut back the flap made by the diaphragm, until 3–4 thin white bones are visible.

(3) With the point of the knife (B), lift out the first 2 or 3 bones, which will be easy. Leave the more firmly attached ones till later.

(4) Cut along the joints between the ribs and the breast bone, marked by knife (C), along the dotted line. Remove each rib as shown by knife (D).

(5) Make another cut along the breast bone as shown by knife (E). Remove the remaining flexible ribs and any other bones.

(6) Spread the stuffing, using recipe on this or on page 176.

(7) Roll and tie.

1 Right

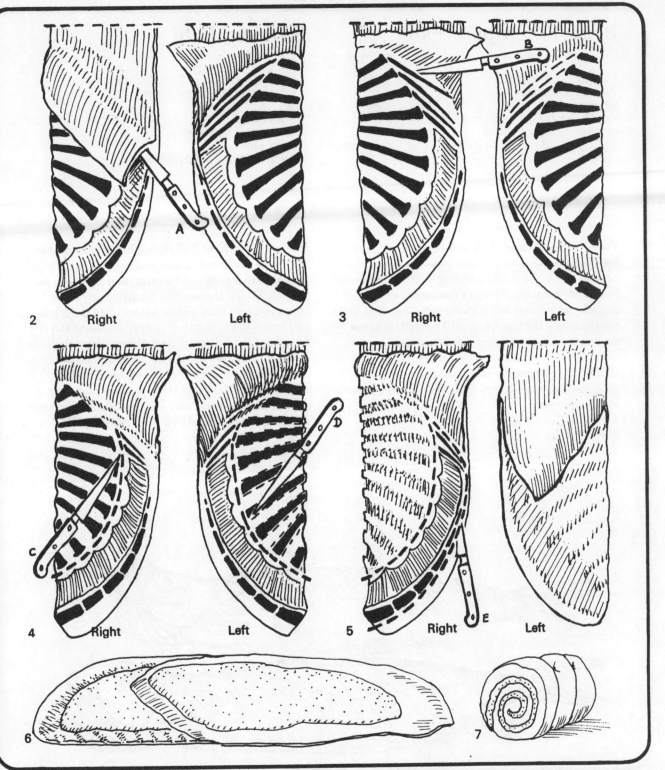

2   Right   Left   3   Right   Left

4   Right   Left   5   Right   Left

6   7

Bloater or Kipper Pâté

1 bloater, or 1 kipper
2–3 oz softened butter
lemon juice
salt and freshly ground pepper
pinch cayenne or nutmeg

Pour boiling water over the fish and let it stand for ten minutes. Remove the flesh from the bones and pound, mince or liquidise, adding butter, lemon juice and seasoning. Mix to a fine paste, and remove any whiskery bones left sticking out. Pack into little pots and fork the top. Chill until needed; it keeps several days in the refrigerator.

☐ *The humble kipper or bloater makes a very good pâté; you can eat it for breakfast, lunch or tea, or for a starter at dinner.*

For 4

Buckling Pâté

2 smoked buckling, or 1 smoked mackerel
2 slices white bread, crusts removed
milk
1 clove garlic
2–3 oz butter, softened
juice of ½ lemon
salt and freshly ground pepper

Remove the skin and all the visible bones from the fish. Soak the bread in milk and squeeze dry. Pound the garlic in a pestle and mortar, add the bread and the fish. Pound thoroughly, removing any little bones you may have missed before. Add the butter and lemon juice, plenty of pepper and some salt if necessary. Pound again, pack the mixture into little pots, and chill. Serve with hot toast and butter. This keeps several days in the refrigerator. It is surprisingly rich and a little goes a long way, but it is quite delicious and very easy to make. If you have a liquidiser you can make it even more rapidly.

For 4

MEAT

Meat

Always be extra nice and good-tempered in the butcher's shop; it really is worth being good friends with the man who sells you your meat. He is the person to steer you clear of bargain cuts that are a maze of bones and gristle, he will show you both sides of a piece of stewing steak before wrapping it up. He will advise you which piece of the animal would be most suitable, if you tell him what you want the meat for. He is also more likely to be prepared to do tedious work in the way of boning, mincing and cutting a joint just so, if he is your friend and sees that you care, and if you make a point of going into the shop when it is not particularly busy.

When choosing meat there are several things to bear in mind. Most carcasses have been frozen or chilled but reach the shop soon after slaughter, and in this short time the freezing, which is done fast and at a very low temperature, does not affect the juiciness of the meat. But what you do not want to carry home in your shopping bag is something that has been sitting in cold storage for weeks; nothing dries meat up so thoroughly, and the fat becomes granular.

New Zealand lamb has of course been frozen, but it is increasingly good as transport gets faster, and is particularly worth buying from October to Christmas, when their lambs are slaughtered and at their best. English lamb, which is slaughtered between three and five months old, is in season from May or even earlier in the year, to September/October; it is expensive but absolutely the best there is.

Avoid any butcher who has everything in the shop already hacked into tiny pieces; these pieces get drier and stringier with every hour they sit around. Better to make for the shop that has whole carcasses hanging up, even if it means waiting a bit longer for the piece you want. Beware also of any chops, steak or liver pre-packed in a cardboard tray; it may be convenient to carry home, but it will have extracted every last drop of juice from the meat by the time it gets there. Since the true art of butchery seems to be on the wane, it is as well to be equipped with the knowledge of a few boning methods, and the equipment with which to do it. A cleaver may make an unsuitable wedding present, but it is useful if you have forgotten to ask the butcher to cut up the bones and find they won't go in the pan; the flat sides can be used for beating steaks, pork fillet etc. A boning knife, having an extremely tough, narrow blade, can be slipped easily round complicated bones to pare away all the meat. A good sharpener and a set of straight-sided, sharp-pointed French knives, a carving knife and fork, plus some metal skewers for securing boned meat are the only other vital pieces of equipment, but a ham knife is useful if you are in the habit of buying large hams or pieces of gammon. Keep your knives razor sharp (a carbon steel is very good for this) and have them re-ground if possible about once a year. Little tungsten-steel wheel knife-sharpeners are not recommended because they leave a thin fragile edge that bends over as soon as you use any pressure. Table-sharpeners and electric knife-sharpeners are fine, provided you use them with care. When using a steel, keep the blade of the knife rather flat against it or you will be bending the edge backwards and forwards with every stroke, and weakening it. Carbon steel knives are still the easiest to sharpen; keep them bright with scouring powder and a cork or with harsh plastic wool.

Some offal, for example fry and chitterlings, is hard to buy and disappearing fast, especially in the South of England, where it is also almost impossible to buy mutton.

Stews, daubes and casseroles almost always make use of the cheaper cuts of meat, which are best bought in a piece and cut up at home, when every morsel of sinew and gristle can be carefully trimmed away; these stringy bits never really become tender and make an otherwise good stew seem less of a treat. Shin, oxtail, ox-tongue and salt-beef, especially brisket, are often disappointingly tough and the reason is almost always the same — undercooking; they must be simmered very gently for up to four hours or even longer, and plenty of time must be allowed for this. Since most daubes and casseroles reheat well, it is a very good idea to cook them the day before, so hungry people won't be kept waiting about for the oxtail to get tender. It also gives you a chance to remove all the fat from the top, before reheating. This fat, clarified, can sometimes be used for dripping (page 220).

Cuts of Meat — Beef, Veal, Pork, Lamb and Mutton

This is an attempt to sort out the confusion caused by the names given by butchers and cookery books to different cuts of meat. A basic understanding of how meat carcasses are divided up is half the battle. The names of the cuts tend to differ according to the species which is misleading as in fact *basically,* all cuts are the same. For example — *breast* of lamb and *brisket* of beef are both cut from the carcass in exactly the same way, they have the same basic qualities and need similar cooking and preparation. But they sound as though they were totally different.

The butcher first removes the head, feet and tail, then splits the carcass in half down the backbone. Then each half is quartered across the base of the ribs, giving two hindquarters and two forequarters.

The Hindquarters

Most of the best meat in all animals comes from the hindquarters. The best meat being the tenderest, least bony and least fatty and therefore the most expensive.

There are two main cuts, the *LEG* and the *LOIN*. The leg is divided from the loin just above the tail where the pelvis joins the backbone.

The legs of VEAL, PORK, LAMB and MUTTON are usually halved to make smaller joints, the best half being the top half which is called (confusingly to some people) the *leg fillet*. The lower half is cheaper and is called the *shank end* or knuckle.

Legs of BEEF are cut differently. The back or round of the leg consists of the *silverside* which is outside, and the *topside* which is inside. The front of the leg is called *top rump* or thick flank. (Thick flank describes it better than top rump, but they are both the same thing and not to be confused with plain *rump* adjoining the loin which is yet another cut). The *aitchbone* consists of the top ends of both topside and silverside and a large lump of pelvic bone, and is a very tasty roast. The lower end of the leg is quite simply called leg and is used for stews. Topside, silverside and top rump are economic slow roasts or braising pieces and can be cut to any weight; they are sold boneless. The *loin* of an animal is where the best meat comes from. It is the lower, rib-less part of the backbone. The part nearest the pelvis is called the *rump* from which *chump chops* of LAMB, PORK and VEAL are cut, as well as *rump steak* for grilling, from BEEF. Running all along the loin, close to the spine, is the tender *fillet*. Fillet of pork is called *tenderloin* and is only cut from very large pigs. The same applies to *lamb fillet*. By far the most expensive part of any animal, the fillet is cut out in one piece by continental and expensive butchers but left in by cheaper English butchers. The *beef fillet* is cut into: rump fillets, Châteaubriands, tournedos and filets mignons. It is also sold whole, for instance for filet en croûte. (See the Beef chart.)

Loins of VEAL, PORK and LAMB can be sold in one piece, whole or boned, and usually including the kidneys. The loin is also cut up for *loin chops* or sold as a *saddle*, which is cut from a whole carcass (and includes both sides) before it is split down the backbone. This is usually done with lamb and mutton.

Loin of BEEF is called *sirloin* and the rib end is called *wing rib*. Porterhouse and T-bone steaks are cut from here.

The Forequarters

These consist mainly of *ribs, shoulders* and *neck*. Also forming part are: the *breast* (or *brisket*) lying between the front legs, and the *belly, flank* or *skirt* running from breast to hind legs. *The ribs* are mainly divided into two. The *best end* nearest the hindquarters, and the *middle*, which lie beneath the shoulder blades. Again confusingly, in the case of VEAL, LAMB and MUTTON, they are called *best end of neck and middle neck*. They are nothing to do with the neck (which is also called *scrag*) but are ribs, and from them come *cutlets*. The best cutlets come from the best end of neck and cost more than middle neck cutlets, which are better for stewing or braising. Remember that veal and lamb chops and cutlets are trimmed of fat and bone before sale and therefore work out more expensive than the price per pound of the part they come from. These same two cuts in the case of PORK are called *fore rib* and *spare rib* (which is beneath the shoulder). In the case of BEEF these same ribs are divided into three main cuts called in order of quality, *fore rib* (adjoining the wing ribs), *middle rib*, and *chuck*. *Fore rib* is also called *chine* and can be roasted, the other rib cuts are usually cheaper and used for pot roasts, braising, stews etc. *Top ribs* are a cheaper, lower part of fore ribs. Other names which crop up in these parts are *oven busters, flat ribs, back ribs* and *Jacob's ladder*. They are very tasty, but need very slow cooking. They include a lot of fat and bone, which can be removed by the butcher.

The shoulders of VEAL, LAMB and MUTTON include the top bone of the foreleg, and the shoulder blade. They are cut like large discs from the rib-cage. They are cheap, being bony. With PORK, the shoulder is cut only to include the shoulder blade and is known as the *blade bone*. The top bone of the leg is called the *hand* and is cut with a piece of the neck called the *spring* to form a very cheap and awkward joint known as the *hand and spring* (see pork chart). With BEEF the shoulder is boned right out, and the meat sold with *chuck* as *blade* for stewing, or pot roasting. The top bone of the foreleg is sometimes boned out and the cut is sold as *leg tops* or *leg-of-mutton* cut (more confusion). The rest of the foreleg is sold for stewing and is known as *shin*.

The *neck* or *scrag*, or in beef, *clod* and *sticking*, are all the same thing, and sold for stews.

The *breast*, or *brisket*, is a very good cheap cut, and consists of the breast bone, with the ends of the ribs that join on to it, or are in its neighbourhood. This cut in PORK is the *thick end of belly*.

The *belly, flank* or *skirt*, is very cheap. In the case of VEAL, LAMB and MUTTON, it tends to be sold either as part of the breast, or as a flap on the loin. With PORK and BEEF it is sold for sausages, pies, mince, stews. It includes a lot of fat. Pork belly is sold salted and fresh.

All *feet* or *trotters* are good sources of gelatine, for consommés and pies.

Beef

1 Leg ** (for stews)
2 Top Rump *** (or Thick Flank, for pot-roasting)
3 Round
3a Topside *** (buttock steak from here for pot-roasting)
3c Aitchbone ** (usually included with topside or silverside)
4 Rump **** (grilling steak)
5 Fillet ***** (sometimes sold as one piece)
5a Rump Fillet *****
5b Chateaubriand *****
5c Tournedos *****
5d Filet Mignon *****
7 Wing Rib ****
8 Skirt * (for stews)
9 Kidney * (and beef suet)
10 Flank * (sold boned for stews and pies and salted for boiling, also for sausages)
11 Forerib *** (or Chine, also sold boned and rolled and as entrecote steaks ****)
12 Middle Rib ** (or Back Rib, for braising and pot-roasting)
12a Top Rib **
12b Flat Ribs ** (or oven-busters, for slow braising)
13 Brisket * (also sold boned and rolled and salted for boiling. Sometimes includes lower ends of clod, chuck, and flat ribs.
14 Shin * (for beef tea and stock)
15 Chuck ** (sold boned, for stewing, braising or pot-roasting)
15a Top Legs ** (or Leg-of-Mutton cut)
15b Flat Ribs **
16 Neck * (or Sticking, for stewing)
17 Clod * (for stewing)
17b Part of Clod sometimes sold with brisket

HINDQUARTER
FOREQUARTER

Beef

Q Quartering Line
1 Leg *
2 Top Rump *** (or Thick Flank)
3 Round
3b Silverside *** (sold salted for
    boiling : also for braising
    and pot-roasting)
3c Aitchbone ** (cheap because
    high proportion of bone)
4 Rump **** (grilling steak)
4a Layer of fat (Cod Fat) good
    for dripping
6 Sirloin **** (including Porter-
    house steaks for roasting, also
    sold boned and rolled)
7 Wing Rib **** (also sold boned
    and rolled for roasting and as
    T-bone and entrecote steaks)
8 Skirt * (or goose)
8a Cod Fat (see **4a**)
10 Flank **
11 Fore Rib ***
12 Middle Rib ** (or Back Rib)
12a Top Rib **
12b Flat Ribs ** (sometimes
    sold with brisket)
13 Brisket *
14 Shin *
15 Chuck **
15a Top Legs ** (or Leg-of-
    Mutton cut)
15b Flat Ribs ** (sometimes sold
    with brisket)
15c Blade **
16 Neck * (or Sticking)
17 Clod *
17b part of Clod sometimes sold
    with brisket.

Prices

* cheap : stew, mince
** middling : stew, braise
*** expensive : pot-roast
**** very expensive⎫
***** astronomical ⎭ roast, grill

Note that cheap cuts come mainly
from the forequarters and bellies,
expensive cuts mainly from the
hindquarters. Some butchers buy
only hindquarters for this reason.

Also sold cheaply : Ox cheek
(brawn), heart, tongue, tail, kidney,
liver (rather strong-tasting), tripe,
feet (or cowheels, very gelatinous—
for brawn)

Pork

Q Quartering line. Above : hind-quarter. Below : forequarter
1 Feet * (trotters, sold fresh or salted)
2 Leg ***
2a Knuckle * (sometimes sold with feet)
3 Leg Fillet *** (includes middle cut)
4 Tail *
5a Belly : thin end * (sold fresh or salted)
5b Belly : middle *
5c Belly : thick end **
6 Loin ****
6a Tenderloin *** (usually from larger bacon pigs)
6b Chump Chops ****
6c Hind Loin **** (chops)
6d Kidney *
7 Fore Loin or Best End *** (usually sold as chops)
8 Spare Ribs ** (sold whole for roasting or as cheap chops)
8a Blade Bone **
9 Hand * (sold fresh or salted, good in pies. Can be roasted)
10 Spring * (as for Hand)

Pork

Q   Quartering line
1   Feet *
2   Leg ***
2a Knuckle *
3a Middle Cut ****
3b Leg Fillet ***
4   Tail *
5a Belly : thin end *
5b Belly : middle *
5c Belly : thick end **
6   Loin ****
7   Fore Loin or Best End ***
8   Spare Ribs **
8a Blade Bone **
9   Hand *
10 Spring *
11 Head *

Prices
* cheap : boiling, pies, sausages
** middling : slow roast
*** expensive ⎫
**** very expensive ⎭ grill or roast
Also sold cheaply : pig's head, heart,
tongue, liver, sweetbreads, ears.

Veal

Q Quartering line
1 Knuckle ** (Osso Buco)
2 Leg Fillet **** (Escalopes)
3 Loin ***
3a Loin Flap (sometimes sold with loin or with breast)
3b Chump Chops ***
3c Loin Chops ***
3d Kidney ***
4 Breast * (can be boned, stuffed and rolled)
5 Best End of Neck ** (sold as cutlets or carré)
6 Middle neck * (cutlets)
7 Scrag *
8 Part of Shoulder

Also sold, but expensive : liver, kidneys

Q Quartering line
1 Knuckle **
2 Leg Fillet ****
3 Loin ** (sold with kidneys)
3a Loin Flap
4 Breast *
5 Best End of Neck **
6 Middle Neck *
7 Scrag *
8 Shoulder ** (can be boned, stuffed and rolled)

Prices
* cheap : pies, ragouts and stews
** middling : blanquettes, roasts
*** expensive } grill, roast, fry
**** very expensive } (escalopes)

Also sold cheaply : calves' head, tongue, brains, feet, sweetbreads, heart, tripe

Lamb

Q Quartering line
1 Leg ***
1a Half Leg, shank end ***
1b Half Leg, fillet end ***
2a Chump Chops ***
2b Loin chops ** (sold with kidneys)
2c Loin Flap (sold with loin or breast)
2d Kidney **
3 Breast *
4 Best End of Neck ** (also sold as cutlets ***)
5 Middle Neck ** (also sold as cutlets and carré)
6 Part of shoulder
7 Neck * (Scrag)

Q Quartering line
1 Leg ***
1a Half Leg, shank end ***
1b Half Leg, fillet end ***
2 Loin *** (includes kidneys)
3 Breast * (can be boned, stuffed and
  rolled for roasting, also for soups and
  stews)
4 Best End of Neck **
5 Middle Neck **
6 Shoulder ** (can be boned, stuffed,
  rolled, or roasted whole)
7 Neck * (Scrag)

Q Quartering line
1 Legs *** (cut like this when a Saddle
  is required)
2 Saddle **** (includes kidneys and
  chump chops)
4 Best End of Neck **
5 Middle Neck **
6 Shoulders **
7 Neck * (Scrag. When combined with
  Best End and Middle Neck is a
  Target)

Q Quartering line
1 Haunch ****
2 Loin *** (Haunch and Loin together
  are a Baron of Lamb or Mutton)

Prices
* cheapest : stew and braise
** middling : braise and slow roast
*** expensive } grill and roast
**** very expensive

Also sold : Head, heart, tongues, brains,
liver, tails, feet, and sweetbreads

Aitchbone of Beef

This is a very large joint, consisting of rump, topside, silverside and brisket. While the quality of the meat on this cut is not as fine as best rump, fillet or sirloin, it does cost far less than half as much per pound, and is very well worth buying for large family dinners or informal parties. It can be eaten hot or cold.

A small aitchbone weighing ten pounds will feed at least ten people; when trimmed it will weigh about eight pounds. Keep the bones and trimmings removed by the butcher to make stock.

Preheat oven to Reg 7/425°. Rub the aitchbone with oil and garlic if liked. Put into the very hot oven, reducing the heat to Reg 4/350° after 20 minutes. Cook 2¼ hours, basting from time to time. There is a large amount of dripping from this joint for roast potatoes, and very good juices for gravy; because it is such a large joint it is juicier.

Serves 10–15 according to size

Boiled Beef and Carrots

4–5 lbs salt beef (brisket or silverside) tied firmly
 with string
1½–2 lbs large carrots, scraped and halved
3–4 Spanish onions, peeled
3–4 turnips, peeled
bouquet garni
a few peppercorns
dumplings (see page 57) (optional)

Always check with the butcher to see if the beef needs soaking, and if so soak overnight. Put it in a large saucepan with any bones that the butcher may have included, barely cover with cold water and bring it slowly to the boil. Skim thoroughly and add half the vegetables and the herbs and peppercorns. Cover and simmer very gently for 2½–3 hours, longer if the meat is particularly tough. Taste the liquid occasionally, and if it is too salt add more water.

Cook the potatoes and fresh vegetables in with it for the last 25–30 minutes and, if you like, add dumplings too.
Serve the beef with the freshly cooked vegetables, dumplings and some of the broth in which it cooked. Keep the rest of the broth for soup.

For 8

Brisket in Beer

3–4 lbs brisket of beef, rolled and tied (fresh, not
  salted)
6 slices streaky bacon
1 lb onions, sliced finely
½ pint brown ale, ½ pint good stock and ¼ pint wine
  vinegar, heated together
salt and pepper
bayleaf

Take a casserole with a lid, large enough to hold all
the ingredients. Line the bottom of it with the bacon,
then put in the meat, pack the onions all around, add
salt and pepper and the bayleaf. Pour over the
stock, beer and vinegar, heated first. Cover tightly
and cook at Reg 1½/290° for 3–3½ hours. This is
very good cold and the remaining stock makes
delicious soup.

For 6–8

Carbonnade Flamande

1¾ lbs chuck steak
dripping
2 large onions, finely sliced
½ pint Guinness or brown ale
salt and freshly ground pepper
bayleaf, sprig of thyme, pinch nutmeg

Cut the trimmed beef into large cubes. Heat the
dripping in a flame-proof casserole, and brown the
meat really well all over, so that it has quite a crust
on the outside. Remove the pieces to a dish and add
the finely sliced onions to the dripping, adding more
if necessary. Fry several minutes until the onions
are nicely browned. Remove them and put them with
the beef while you pour in three-quarters of the beer;
let it froth up, scraping the bottom of the pan with
a wooden spoon until you have loosened all the
sediment. Return the beef and onions, add salt,
pepper, herbs and nutmeg and simmer covered on
top of the cooker, or in a slow oven, Reg 2/300°, for
2½–3 hours, adding a little water if the gravy gets
too thick.

Five minutes before serving add the rest of the beer,
taste for seasoning and simmer five minutes more.
Serve with boiled potatoes and drink beer with it.
A salad of lettuce eaten off the same plate afterwards benefits from the juices of the carbonnade.

For 4–5

A very simple Beef Stew

3 lbs stewing beef, leg or chuck
4 oz flour
salt and freshly ground pepper
1 pint best beef stock, or use plain water
oil and dripping to brown the meat
24 button onions
24 slender carrots
½ lb button mushrooms (optional)

Trim any gristle or fat from the meat and cut it into cubes. Season the flour generously and roll the meat in it. Melt one tablespoon of dripping and one of oil in a flameproof casserole, large enough for all the meat and vegetables, and brown the meat very thoroughly. If any flour remains, brown it, too, in a little more fat. Heat the stock or water and pour on to the meat. If you like lots of gravy add a further ¼ pint. When it is all gently simmering, cover and transfer to a very low oven, Reg 1/275°. After one hour put the little onions and carrots, carefully cleaned and scraped, on top of the meat. Half an hour later add the mushrooms. Depending on the quality of the meat, two hours should be enough to cook this stew, but longer won't hurt.

Parsley dumplings (page 57) added 20 minutes before eating the stew are a very pretty alternative to potatoes.

□ *This stew tastes really rich, especially if proper beef stock is used; it is hard to believe there is no wine or garlic in it. The gravy should be smooth and velvety and a good colour.*

Beef Olives

1 lb topside or rump steak, sliced thin
3 oz breadcrumbs
1 dessertspoon parsley, chopped
1 oz suet, finely chopped
2 anchovies, chopped
1 teaspoon lemon juice
1 egg
salt and freshly ground pepper
1 oz dripping
1 oz flour
1 pint fresh stock or water

Beat the slices of beef to flatten them. Cut them into pieces about $3 \times 1\frac{1}{2}$ inches. Make a stuffing with the breadcrumbs, parsley, suet, anchovies, lemon juice, beaten egg, salt and pepper. Lay a little of this on each strip of beef, roll up and tie with a piece of string or thread. Heat the dripping in a frying pan and brown the beef rolls all over. Remove and drain on kitchen paper, while you sprinkle the flour into the pan, brown it, then add hot water or stock gradually, stirring to avoid lumps. Bring to the boil, season, return the meat and simmer uncovered for one hour, turning the rolls occasionally. When tender remove the string or thread from the olives and put them with the gravy into a hot dish.

For 4

Beef Goulash

2 lbs stewing beef, leg or chuck
2 lbs onions
1 lb tomatoes, skinned and quartered
2 dessertspoons paprika
8 peppercorns
salt
dripping

Trim the beef carefully and cut into cubes. Peel and quarter the onions, or cut into eights if very large. Fry them in two tablespoons of dripping in a flameproof casserole, put them aside and brown the beef, adding more dripping if necessary. Return the onions, sprinkle with paprika and stir in well. Add the tomatoes, peppercorns and salt to taste. Cover and put in a low oven, Reg 2/325°, for two hours or until tender.

This is very good reheated the following day. The juice from the tomatoes and from the meat and onions, which is extracted with the help of the paprika, provides an astounding amount of delicious thick gravy.

Serve with plain boiled potatoes, on to which you can sprinkle some dill seeds if liked.

For 4

Chilli Con Carne

2 lbs beef, skirt or chuck
1 lb red kidney beans
2 large onions, chopped
olive oil
2 teaspoons ground turmeric
1 tablespoon ground coriander
1–2 teaspoons ground chilli, according to how hot you like it
1 teaspoon fresh green chilli, chopped (optional)
2 cloves garlic, crushed
1 lb fresh tomatoes, peeled and chopped
salt and freshly ground pepper

Soak the beans overnight. Fry the chopped onions in olive oil in a flameproof casserole, turn up the heat and add the meat either cut in one-inch cubes, or minced if you like. Fry fairly fast for five to ten minutes, scraping the sediment from the bottom of the casserole. Add the spices, garlic and chilli and continue to fry, stirring, for several minutes. Then add the peeled chopped tomatoes, salt and pepper and simmer, covered, until the meat is tender, about two hours if it is cubed, less if it is minced. Meanwhile the beans should be put in a large pan of cold water and brought slowly to the boil; add salt after one hour. They take $1\frac{1}{2}$–2 hours to cook and can be combined with the meat half an hour before serving, or served separately. A dish of plain white rice is a good foil to the dark beans and hot beef stew.

For 6–8

Pot-au-Feu

3 lbs topside of beef
1 clove garlic
2 oz lard or back pork fat
1 lb beef marrow bones, broken up
small tablespoon salt
6 carrots ⎫
3 turnips ⎬ peeled
1 parsnip ⎭
1 large onion, stuck with cloves
4 leeks, 1 stick celery
small bunch parsley
slices of French bread

Put the beef, stuck with slivers of garlic for flavour, and little pieces of lard which keep it moist, into four or five pints of cold water. Add the bones and bring to the boil. Turn down the heat at once; skim and keep skimming until no more scum rises, and then add the salt and vegetables, the leeks, celery and parsley tied in a bundle.

When the liquid comes to the boil again, turn the heat very low, so the liquid is just moving or trembling and simmer four or five hours. Throw out the bones. Take out the beef and vegetables and keep them hot. Let the liquid stand for five minutes, and skim off all the fat. A good housewife clarifies this to use for frying (see page 220). Now put a scalded fine cloth in a wire sieve, over a bowl and strain the liquid through this. Taste for seasoning and put to keep hot. Put some pieces of French bread, previously toasted, on a plate, sprinkle them with some of the fat from the top of the soup, heat them under the grill and serve these with the soup. Serve the beef and vegetables as a second course with some sea salt crystals to hand round, or aïoli (page 176) or horseradish (page 179).

The French very often sieve the vegetables and serve them as a purée. It is true that after four or five hours they are pretty soggy, so it is a good idea to add fresh ones about one hour before the end, and to boil some potatoes separately to serve with the beef. If you have a very large pot, you can also include a large boiling fowl, to make a good meal for about 12.

☐ *The most important thing about a pot-au-feu is that it should be cooked very, very slowly once the broth has been skimmed and the vegetables added.*

For 6

Oxtail Stew

2 small or 1 very large oxtail, jointed
dripping, or butter and oil for browning
seasoned flour
4 oz salt pork or bacon, cut in cubes
glass red wine (optional)
2–3 large onions, peeled and stuck with cloves
2 cloves garlic, bouquet garni
2 tablespoons or 1 small tin tomato purée
1 pint beef stock, water or bouillon
1 lb carrots, 1 turnip, 1 lb leeks
4–5 sticks celery, seasoning

Start early in the morning by soaking the pieces of oxtail in cold salt water, for 2–4 hours. Remove and dry them well. Prepare the vegetables, cutting up everything but the leeks. Preheat the oven to Reg 2/300°. Roll the pieces of meat in four or five tablespoons of well-seasoned flour until they are thoroughly coated. Heat the dripping or butter and oil in a large flameproof casserole and toss the bacon or pork cubes in it until the fat starts to run. Remove them, and brown the oxtail pieces very well all over. Pour in the wine and let it bubble up, then add the pork, onions, garlic, herbs, half the carrots, the turnip and the warmed water or stock mixed with the tomato purée. Bring slowly to the boil and put the casserole, covered, into the oven. Cook at Reg 2/300° for one hour, then at Reg 1½/290° for a further 2–3 hours.

Three quarters of an hour before serving skim the fat off the top of the stew, check the seasoning and add the remaining vegetables. Continue cooking until they are tender. Skim again before serving with potatoes and/or dumplings (page 57).

☐ *This is not a traditional English oxtail stew and has a richer flavour.*

For 4–6

Corned Beef Hash

8 oz tin of corned beef, cut into chunks
1 lb potatoes, peeled, boiled and cut in cubes
3–4 onions, sliced and fried golden in lard
lard or dripping
salt, freshly ground pepper, and a dash of Worcester sauce

Mix all the ingredients together with a fork, in a large bowl. Heat a couple of tablespoons of lard or dripping in the biggest frying pan you have. Tip the hash into the hot fat and flatten it gently. Cook for about five minutes, shaking the pan from time to time. When a crust has formed over the bottom of the hash put a large flat plate over the frying pan and turn the whole thing over. Put another tablespoon of lard or dripping in the now empty frying pan. Slide the hash back into the pan with the crust now on top. Cook another five minutes, until there is a rustling crust on the bottom. Serve in big slices; it should be lovely and moist inside. It will keep warm in a low oven for a while without going soggy.

For 4

Steak and Kidney Pudding

For the pudding:
8 oz self-raising flour
4 oz shredded beef suet
salt
water

For the filling.
1 lb decent stewing steak
3 lambs kidneys or 4–6 oz ox kidney
2 oz seasoned flour
stock
1 medium-sized onion, chopped
¼ lb mushrooms, sliced (if liked)

Trim the meat and cut it into neat pieces. Skin, core, and slice the kidneys. Roll meat and kidney in seasoned flour. Add onion and mushrooms (if liked). Make the pastry by mixing suet, flour and salt with a little cold water. Roll it out and, keeping a piece for the lid, line a greased pudding basin. (This basin should be large enough for the pudding to increase in size a little during cooking.) Put in the meat, etc., adding a little more seasoning and cold stock almost to cover. Shape the lid, damp the edges of the pastry, and seal firmly. The pudding should be at least one inch below the top of the basin. Cover with greased paper, then foil, or a cloth, and tie well (see page 205). Cook in a large pan of boiling water (with a lid) for 5 hours. Keep the water boiling and well topped up. You can cook it half one day and half the next if necessary. Serve it turned out of the basin with more gravy and plain boiled potatoes, carrots or cabbage, and mustard.

☐ *Some people prefer to leave out the onions and mushrooms. Cook it less long if you use better quality meat.*

For 4–6

Hamburgers

1–2 slices home-made type bread
1 lb minced beef
1 small onion, chopped
1 clove garlic, finely chopped
parsley, thyme, pinch nutmeg
salt and freshly ground pepper
oil and butter for frying

Soak the bread in water, squeeze dry and crumble into a bowl. Add the meat, onions, garlic, herbs and seasoning and mix thoroughly. Shape into 12 small, flat round cakes on a floured board. Heat oil and butter in a large frying pan over a moderate heat and fry the hamburgers for three or four minutes on each side, depending on how well you like them cooked. They can be pink and juicy inside, or brown right through. Serve with fried onions, or plain, or with fresh tomato sauce (page 185). They are much cheaper than frozen ones, a good deal less than half the price, and they taste better.

For 4

Poor Man's Cassoulet

2 ½ lbs meaty end of fresh belly of pork
1 lb dried haricot beans, soaked overnight
1 onion, peeled
1 lb tomatoes, skinned and chopped
1 clove garlic, crushed
salt and freshly ground pepper

Pork Kebabs

2 lbs leg of pork, off the bone
oregano
fresh lemon juice
freshly ground pepper
olive oil
salt

The pork belly should be boned and cut in one-inch slices. Roast these slices in a medium hot oven, Reg 5/375°, for 15 minutes. Put the beans in a pan with the onion and cover by an inch with cold water. Bring to the boil and simmer 45 minutes. Put the tomatoes in a casserole with the lightly roasted pork and its juices, the crushed clove of garlic, the beans, onion and half the liquid in which they were cooked. Add salt and pepper and cook in a low oven, Reg 3/325°, for two hours, keeping closely covered. This is better if made the day before and reheated. The juice should be rich and creamy.

For 6

Even in the cheapest Greek restaurants they do use leg of pork rather than a cheaper cut, because it is so much better.

Cut the pork into little cubes and sprinkle liberally with oregano, lemon juice and pepper. Allow it to soak up these flavours for a couple of hours, turning the cubes over from time to time. Thread the cubes on skewers and shake off as much lemon juice as you can. Brush with oil and grill fast for five minutes, turning frequently. Sprinkle with salt and pepper and eat with a salad of green bottled chillies, lettuce and raw onions, and with plain rice. The bottled chillies can be found at most continental provision stores and delicatessens.

For 4–6

Fried Pork Fillet

1 small pork fillet
juice of ½ lemon
salt and freshly ground pepper
butter for frying

Slice the pork fillet into little rounds about quarter of an inch thick. There will seem a lot, but they shrink in cooking. Between two pieces of grease-proof paper beat the little rounds of meat flat with a rolling pin. Season with lemon juice, plenty of fresh ground black pepper and a little salt. Melt the butter in a frying pan, and when it starts to brown slide in half the little escalopes of pork. As soon as the edges become whitish, flip the pieces over. They should fry quite quickly and be delicately browned and juicy after three or four minutes on each side. Slide on to a hot dish and fry the remaining pieces. When they are done and removed to the hot dish, squeeze any remaining lemon juice into the pan and add a little hot water (sherry is good too if you have it). Pour the pan juices over the meat and eat with a carefully made purée of creamy potatoes. These little escalopes are just as good in flavour as veal and much juicier.

☐ *Pork fillet is also called pork tenderloin. It is a totally lean piece of meat, and a good buy because there is no waste at all.*

For 2

Stuffed Pork Fillet

1 small pork fillet (tenderloin)
1 small Italian, or other spicy sausage
2 oz mushrooms, chopped and sweated in butter
1 beaten egg yolk
parsley, chopped
salt and freshly ground pepper
2 rashers streaky bacon
butter for roasting
little dry white wine or cider

Preheat oven to Reg 5/375°. Score the fillet down the middle twice, lengthwise, taking care not to cut right through. You can now flatten it out like an oblong piece of pastry; bang it even flatter with a rolling pin.

Skin the sausage and mix the contents in a bowl with the egg yolk, chopped mushrooms, sweated in butter, chopped parsley and seasoning. Put this stuffing in a line down the middle of the flattened fillet. Fold the fillet over the stuffing and fasten into a long sausage shape with string or toothpicks. Cover the joint, which should be pressed together well, with the bacon slices, rinds removed, to keep the meat moist (see diagram opposite).

Cover with foil and roast with a little butter at Reg 5/375°, for 40–45 minutes, removing the foil for the last ten minutes. Remove the string or toothpicks and cut the meat into little round slices, each prettily enclosing a nugget of stuffing, and serve with a thin gravy made with the pan juices and a little dry white wine or cider. The fillet can be dry if overcooked, but always tastes very delicious.

For 2–3

Salt Pork

Salt Pork with Peas

2 lbs salt pork belly (lean end), skin removed
1 large onion, sliced
6 carrots, sliced lengthwise
2 bayleaves
bunch of parsley and thyme, tied with a thread
8 oz yellow split peas
salt if needed

If you buy salt pork at Sainsbury's or other super-markets, you can be sure it will not be over-salty, because they are consistent about the amount of time the meat stays in the brine. However, many small butchers keep pieces of meat in the brine-tub indefinitely to preserve them; it is essential to find out, when buying from a butcher with a vast brine-tub, just how long each piece of pork has been there, how salty it is, and how long a soaking it will need. Do not be put off by the butcher's suggestion of bringing the meat to the boil in a pan of water and then throwing this water away. This does not work on very salty pork; it does need soaking, overnight at least.

Soak the pork, overnight if necessary. Put it in a large saucepan, cover with cold water and bring to the boil. In the meantime prepare the vegetables. Add them and the herbs to the pork and simmer for two hours, covered. Remove the vegetables and add the split peas to the water; taste for salt and simmer until the peas are cooked, about one hour. Some people put the peas in a cloth bag and hang it over the side of the pan in the water to cook. It does prevent them from dissolving into a mush. If they do disintegrate, strain off the liquid before serving the peas on a dish round the piece of pork.

☐ *This is a filling peasant dish.*

For 6

Boiled Bacon

any cheap cut of green or smoked bacon (½ lb per
    person, more if there is bone or a lot of fat)
2 medium onions per person
3 medium carrots per person
bayleaf, sprig parsley
whole cloves
breadcrumbs
Demerara sugar

Green is milder than smoked, and since only the butcher or grocer know how salty either is (and even he may not), green is less risky, and less likely to need long soaking. Large cuts nearly always need soaking several hours or overnight. The cheapest cuts are hock, which has quite a lot of fat, and collar which is leaner. Hock is better eaten cold; a large piece, weighing eight or nine pounds, is good for parties.

Timing: small pieces, 1–3 lbs, need 1–1½ hours. Large pieces, 3 lbs and over, need 30–35 minutes to the pound. To see if it is cooked, push a skewer into the meat. If it goes in and comes out easily it is ready. Bacon is better slightly over- than under-cooked. Soak the bacon in several changes of water if necessary. Tie firmly with white string if it is a ragged piece. Just cover with cold water, in a pan large enough to hold all the vegetables and herbs. If the piece of bacon is small, 2 lbs and under, put the peeled onions in at the beginning of the cooking, with the herbs; if the piece is large put the herbs in at the start but add the onions 1 hour before the end. Let the water come slowly to the boil, then simmer gently. Add the scraped carrots half an hour before the end of the cooking. At the same time remove the bacon, letting the vegetables go on cooking in the liquid.

Remove the string from the bacon and gently peel away the rind. Criss-cross the fat in a diamond pattern, with lines about an inch apart. Mix equal parts of soft breadcrumbs and Demerara sugar, enough to cover the scored fat. Press the mixture into the fat with your hands. Stick a clove into the centre of each diamond. Put the bacon in an oven-proof dish with two tablespoons of the cooking liquid to prevent it sticking. After 20 minutes in a moderate oven, Reg 5/375°, the sugar and bread-crumbs should have combined to make a firm sweet crust. Serve with the vegetables, drained and arranged on the dish with the bacon, either whole or sliced, and with parsley sauce if liked. Whole boiled potatoes are good with this too, and if you have a good firm variety you can cook them in the bacon stock with the carrots. Keep the stock for pea soup etc.

Pork, Beef or Chicken Korma

1½ lbs pork or beef cut into squares, or 2 lbs raw
  chicken joints
for the marinade:
1 teaspoon ground turmeric
1 clove garlic, crushed
1 5-oz carton plain yoghurt

1 clove garlic, 1 onion
butter for frying, salt
5 whole cloves
5 whole cardamoms
1 cinnamon stick of about 1 inch

Marinate the meat in the yoghurt, mixed with
turmeric and a crushed clove of garlic, for an hour
or more. Slice the onion and the whole clove of
garlic and fry lightly in butter in a flameproof
casserole without browning. Add the spices, fry a
few minutes longer, than add the meat and its
marinade. Season with a little salt.

Cook covered in a slow oven, Reg 2/300°, for 1½
hours for chicken or pork, two hours for beef.

☐ *This curry is absolutely not hot, but is mild and
spicy and very delicious contrasted with a hot one.*

For 4–6

Gratin of Ham and Potatoes

½ large onion, chopped
1 clove garlic, crushed and chopped
nut of butter
1 tablespoon oil
4 oz slice ham
2 eggs
½ pint milk
2 oz Gruyère, grated
1 oz Parmesan, grated
salt, freshly ground pepper and nutmeg
1 lb potatoes

Preheat oven to Reg 5/375°. Heat a little butter and
the olive oil in a small frying pan and soften the
onion and garlic for 10–15 minutes without browning.
Add the ham cut into sticks like large matches,
heat through and keep warm.

Meanwhile beat the eggs into the milk, and add the
grated cheese, salt, pepper and a touch of nutmeg.
Peel the potatoes and grate them coarsely; squeeze
out the water with your hands (there will be more
than you think). Mix the whole lot together in a bowl,
turn it into a buttered oval gratin dish, and dot the
top with butter. Bake in the top of the oven for 30–
35 minutes; finish off by browning under the grill.

☐ *This is a very good lunch for a winter's day.*

For 4

Roast Best End of Lamb

Epigrams of Lamb

1 lb breast of lamb
1½ oz butter, melted
1 egg, beaten
pinch thyme
1 cupful fresh white breadcrumbs
salt and freshly ground pepper
Béarnaise sauce (page 184), or tomato sauce
(page 185)

A best end usually consists of six or seven chops joined together, so one is enough for three people. Get the butcher to chop and chine it, and to tear off the tough skin.

Preheat the oven to Reg 3/325°. Rub the fat with a mixture of oil and lemon juice, or oil and salt, and insert slivers of garlic and rosemary here and there. Roast at Reg 3/325° for about one hour or at Reg 5/375° for 45 minutes. Make a gravy from the pan juices and stock or white wine. Carve the meat into juicy, pink little chops, and serve with Pommes Rissolées (page 163).

For 3

Remove the bones, gristle and some of the fat from the cooked lamb while it is still warm, and cut into neat fingers or squares when cold. Mix the melted butter with the beaten egg, thyme and seasoning. Dip each piece of lamb into this mixture, then into fresh breadcrumbs.

Grill under a moderate heat until browned both sides, and serve with Béarnaise or tomato sauce. They make crisp little morsels which should be enjoyed by children.

☐ *This dish is quite luxurious and rich, and yet is made out of the most humble piece of meat that has already done a stint in the cooking of Scotch Broth (see page 14). It is definitely better if it is eaten fairly soon after it comes out of the broth.*

For 2–3

Shoulder of Lamb with Avgolemono Sauce

1 shoulder lamb
4 cloves garlic
2 lbs broad beans
2 egg yolks
juice 1 lemon
salt and pepper
a little chicken stock
butter or oil for roasting

Ask the butcher to chop the shoulder down through the bone, but not right through the meat underneath, to make slices one inch thick. The shoulder is now easy to carve into slices but still in one piece (see diagram). Put in a roasting pan, fat side up, with the peeled cloves of garlic in the cuts. Spread the joint with a little butter or oil, sprinkle with salt and pepper, and roast at Reg 5/375° for $\frac{3}{4}$–1 hour, basting two or three times.

Meanwhile cook the shelled broad beans in boiling salted water and drain, keeping some of the water they cooked in. Beat together the egg yolks and lemon juice and add about half a cup of the bean liquid. When the lamb is cooked remove it from the roasting pan and keep it warm on a dish in the oven. Remove the garlic and skim off the fat from the juices in the pan, before stirring them into the egg and lemon sauce. Put this sauce in a pan over a very low flame, add the broad beans and about two tablespoons of stock, season and thicken very gently — it takes a long time — without ever boiling.

Slice up the shoulder, pour on the sauce, and serve with plain rice or baked potatoes and a simple salad.

☐ *This is a Greek dish and very delicious; the lemon counteracts the richness of a fat shoulder very well.*

For 6

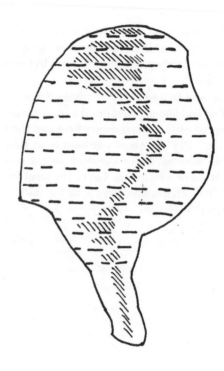

Boiled Leg of Lamb and Caper Sauce

1 large leg New Zealand lamb
1 swede or turnip
1 leek, 1 onion, 2 carrots
2 tablespoons sea salt, less if using ordinary salt
for caper sauce:
salt
1 oz butter, ½ oz flour
3 or 4 tablespoons lamb cooking liquid
1 tablespoon capers
1 tablespoon caper vinegar
thin cream or top of the milk

Cover the leg of lamb with cold water in a large saucepan, and bring it slowly to the boil. Skim impeccably, add the peeled whole vegetables and salt. Simmer, covered, very slowly so the water just turns lazily in the pan, and keep skimmed. It will take 1¾–2 hours. Strain well before serving. Make a sauce with the butter, flour, three to four tablespoons of lamb broth, strained, and the caper vinegar. Add the capers and a little cream, and if you like you can add the onion that cooked with the lamb, chopped fairly small. Season the sauce and serve in a jug: it should be the consistency of cream. Boiled potatoes are best with this dish, or perhaps turnips, cooked in with the meat for the last 25 minutes.

☐ *If you buy New Zealand leg of lamb towards the end of summer it is very cheap and on the large side. Boiled, it tastes almost as good as the mutton that used to be available, and served with caper sauce it is perfect.*

For 6–8

Irish Stew

3 lbs neck of lamb
3 lbs smallish potatoes
1 lb onions, sliced
½ lb carrots, peeled and sliced
2 leeks, cut in one-inch pieces
1 young turnip, peeled and sliced
plenty of salt and freshly ground pepper
parsley, chopped

The usual Irish stew is a very basic dish in which the fat is eaten with the rest. For many people's taste it is too depressing to eat like this. If, however, you put whole potatoes on top of your stew, the fat is absorbed by these and in a curious way it makes them delicious. A wide shallow casserole is better than a deep narrow one, so that the fat can reach all the potatoes.

Peel the potatoes, and cut half of them into thin slices and place in the bottom of a buttered casserole. Put the prepared vegetables on top of them, season and then add the lamb, cut in chops and with all the accessible fat removed. Season again and cover with whole potatoes. Sprinkle with quarter of a pint of water or stock, and put a piece of oiled greaseproof paper over the potatoes. Cover with a tight-fitting lid and bake at Reg 3/325° for 2½ hours. Remove the greaseproof paper. Sprinkle the top with parsley before serving.

For 6–8

Lamb Polo

1 lb dried apricots
2 boned shoulders lamb (ask the butcher to do it for
  you or follow diagram opposite)
4 onions, chopped
4 oz cooking butter (2 oz are for the rice)
2 teaspoons ground coriander
1 teaspoon ground cinnamon
2 teaspoons ground cumin
salt and freshly ground pepper
2 lbs rice

Pour one pint of boiling water over the apricots and allow them to soak for an hour or two. Start cooking the rice in the Persian way (page 166). Trim most of the fat from the meat, and cut it into one-inch squares.

Melt half the butter in a large flameproof casserole, soften the chopped onions and brown lightly, stirring all the time. Turn up the heat and add the lamb. Brown all over very thoroughly and add the spices. Fry them, stirring well, for two or three minutes, then add the apricots with the water in which they soaked, plenty of salt and plenty of pepper. Add enough water just to cover the meat and simmer, covered, for 1½ hours, or until tender, stirring from time to time. Serve with Persian rice.

☐ *This is a Persian recipe; it has a beautiful, spicy, strange flavour and smell. It can well be made the day before as it is improved, if anything, by being kept and reheated.*

For 10–12

Boning a Shoulder (Lamb or Veal)

Place the shoulder cut side up. Take a sharp knife and make three cuts through to the bones as shown in diagram 1 (according to whether it is a right or left hand shoulder). Trim the meat away from the bones as shown in diagram 2. First slide the knife under the top edge of the blade bone, which may be soft gristle in a young animal (shown by dashes) and looking out for the ridge down the centre (shown by dots). Free the meat so that the blade bone can be lifted out. Then sever it at the joint. Free the second and third bones in the same way. (The knife should never go through the skin.) Spread the meat with a suitable stuffing (Spinach Stuffing, page 176, is advised) and fold in the leg flap neatly (diagram 3). Roll it up and tie as shown in diagram 4.

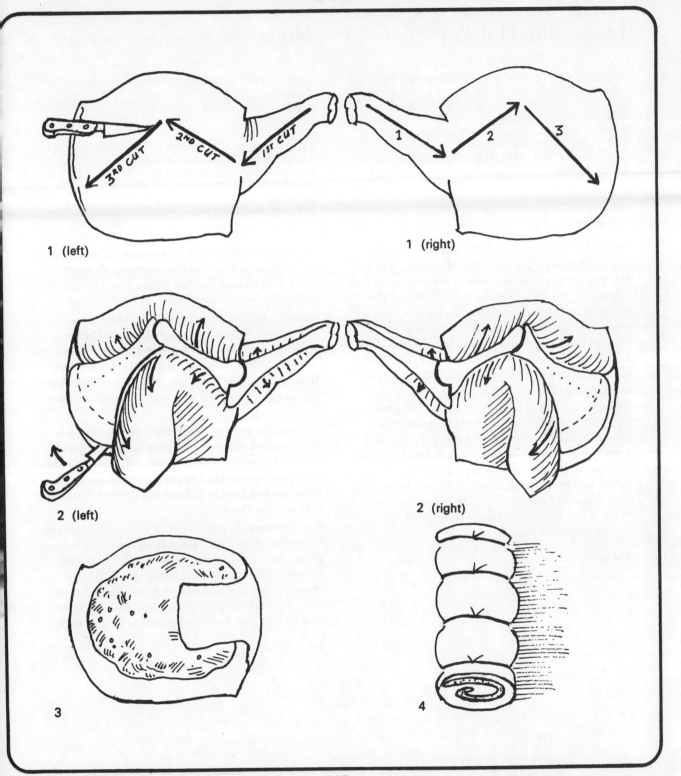

1 (left)

1 (right)

2 (left)

2 (right)

3

4

Lancashire Hot-Pot

2–3 lbs middle neck of lamb, cut into chops and
    trimmed of fat
8 medium potatoes, peeled and thickly sliced
3 medium onions, sliced
3 lambs' kidneys, skinned, cored and sliced
4 oz mushrooms, sliced if large
12 shelled oysters are traditional but not vital
1 oz dripping
1 oz flour
¾ pint water
salt and freshly ground pepper
½ oz butter

Preheat the oven to Reg 3/325°. Make the hot-pot
in a tall round pot, of iron or earthenware. Use half
the butter to grease the inside of the pot, put in half
the sliced potatoes, and season them. Brown the
chops in some hot dripping in a frying pan, and lay
them over the potatoes. Season, and cover with a
layer of onions also fried in dripping, followed by
the kidneys, mushrooms, and oysters if you have
them, seasoning each layer. Finish with a layer of
overlapping slices of potato. Fry the flour in the
frying pan with a little more dripping, and gradually
add ¾ pint boiling water, stirring to remove the
sediment from the bottom of the frying pan. Cook
a few minutes to thicken a little and strain over the
contents of the pot. Season the top layer, dot with
butter and cover. Cook, covered, for two hours, and
for a further ½ hour uncovered to brown the top.
Serve very hot with pickled red cabbage, its
traditional accompaniment.

For 6

Moussaka

1½ lbs cooked lamb or beef, finely chopped or
    minced
3 large onions, sliced
1 lb aubergines
olive oil for cooking
½ pint stock, bouillon or gravy
3 tablespoons tomato purée
salt and freshly ground pepper
for the top:
3 or 4 egg yolks
¾–1 pint seasoned milk

Make the top first, as it takes up to an hour to cook;
it combines so well with the aubergine flavour that
it is worth making this top rather than the alternative Béchamel sauce.

Combine the beaten egg yolks and seasoned milk
and put to thicken in the top of a double boiler,
or bain-marie; don't let the water boil or the sauce
will curdle. Stir with a wooden spoon from time to
time, while you prepare the other ingredients. When
it is like thick custard let it cool and thicken even
further.

Preheat the oven to Reg 4/350°. Meanwhile slice
the unpeeled aubergines thickly on the slant and
fry them gently in plenty of olive oil; they should be
just transparent, not browned. As they cook, lift
them out and line the bottom of a deep oval casserole
with some of them.

Fry the onions in more oil until brown. Put half the
minced meat into the casserole on top of the aubergines, then the onions then more aubergines and
the rest of the meat. Press firmly down. Mix the
tomato purée and seasoning into the heated stock
and pour over the meat. Spoon the custard-like top
over all and cook for about one hour at Reg 4/350°.

For 5–6

Greek Meatballs

1 lb fresh minced beef and lamb, mixed
2 eggs
1 clove garlic, crushed
1 medium onion, finely chopped
handful coriander leaves or parsley, chopped
½ teaspoon cinnamon
1 teaspoon salt and plenty of freshly ground pepper
3-inch piece stale French bread, or thick slice any
   home-made type white bread
butter and oil for frying
milk or water

Put the meat, eggs, garlic, onion, herbs and seasonings in a bowl, and mix. Soften the bread, crusts removed, in milk or water. Squeeze dry and crumble into the mixture. Mix again thoroughly — with your hands is the easiest way. On a floured board roll into walnut sized balls and fry in a mixture of butter and oil for five to six minutes, turning frequently. Serve with a fresh tomato sauce (page 185).

For 4–5

Shepherd's Pie

1½ lbs minced beef, or lamb (fresh or left-over)
1 large onion
1 clove garlic
2 tomatoes
2 carrots
stock, water, parsley, bayleaf, thyme
tablespoon tomato purée
1½ lbs potatoes
¼ pint milk, 1½ ozs butter
salt and pepper
olive oil, or dripping
dessertspoon flour, ½ oz butter, for thickening

Put three or four tablespoons olive oil or dripping in a wide shallow pan and heat gently. Chop the onion and garlic finely and add them to the fat. While they are frying, peel the tomatoes and chop them finely. When the onions start to brown, add the tomatoes and cook fast, stirring, until all the water has evaporated and the sauce starts to brown. Now add the meat and carrots, grated on the coarse side of the grater. Fry fast for ten minutes more, if using raw meat, turning the meat over often.

If using left-over (cooked) meat, warm through gently. Now add half-stock, half-water to come almost to the top of the meat, but not to cover it. Add thyme, salt and pepper, bayleaf, tomato purée and a handful of chopped parsley. Left-over meat needs no further cooking, but if using fresh meat, simmer for an hour and a half, adding more stock as needed and stirring from time to time. Work a dessertspoon of plain flour into a nut of butter (about half an ounce) and drop little pieces of this paste into the mince, stirring, to thicken it. If you thicken it at the beginning it tends to separate and your mince has a lot of Spanish looking tomato-coloured oil on top. After adding the flour, cook on for 20 minutes. Put the meat into a pie dish. Cover with creamy mashed potatoes made exactly as on page 164. Bake in a moderate oven, Reg 5/375°, for 25 minutes until nicely brown and tempting.

For 6

Veal

Blanquette de Veau

2 lbs shoulder or breast of veal
2 bayleaves
12 peppercorns
2 onions, 4 carrots
salt
4 tablespoons good stock (if available)
2 oz butter
1 oz flour
½ lb mushrooms (optional)
2 egg yolks
1 small lemon
4 tablespoons cream

Buying cheap English veal for a blanquette is quite all right as long as it is well trimmed. But this is difficult to do when the meat is raw, even with a very sharp knife, because of the abundant gristle and hidden pipes. However, if you cut it into large pieces — if a shoulder, take out the bone, and if breast cut into three or four chunks — and then blanch it for five or ten minutes and refresh in cold water, this both solidifies the meat and removes some of the scum. The veal can then be trimmed of unwanted pieces and cut into neat shapes. Keep the liquid in which the veal was blanched; together with the bones and trimmings it makes a good jellied stock.

Cut the veal into one-inch squares, removing the fat. Put in a saucepan, cover with cold water, bring to the boil and let it simmer with two bayleaves and a few peppercorns for ¾ hour. Now add the sliced onions, a piece of lemon peel, a few carrots and some salt. Four tablespoons of good stock can also be added at this stage. Simmer on for another 1¼ hours. Melt the butter in another pan, stir in the flour and one pint of the hot veal broth, strained. Add the cleaned mushrooms and cook for ten minutes. Then, off the heat, add the strained pieces of veal, the egg yolks beaten with the juice of a small lemon, a little more stock if needed and the cream. Heat thoroughly, letting the egg yolks thicken slightly, taste for seasoning and serve with a fresh-looking vegetable such as French beans or fresh peas.

For 6

Tripe

Tripe and Onions

2 lbs prepared tripe
3–4 Spanish onions, peeled and sliced
6 bacon rinds, or a small piece of salt pork or ham
bayleaf, mace
enough milk and water, half and half, to cover the
    tripe and onions (1–1 ¼ pints altogether)
salt and freshly ground pepper
2 oz butter
scant 2 oz flour
4 triangular pieces fried bread

Veal tripe is best, but ox-tripe is more commonly sold. It can be bought prepared to varying degrees, so find out from the butcher how much longer it needs to be cooked. It is sold completely raw (don't buy it like this if possible); blanched and scraped; prepared or 'half-cooked' (which is the best way to buy it) and cooked.

If you do buy raw tripe, wash it very well and then blanch it (bring to the boil in salted water and refresh in cold water). Then simmer the blanched tripe for three hours in salted water with carrots, onions, celery, a bayleaf and some peppercorns, by which time it is 'half-cooked'.

Half-cooked tripe is ready to be turned into a stew or braised in a rich sauce.

Fully cooked tripe is often egg-and-breadcrumbed and fried. Tripe should be eaten 'al dente', with a slight bite, like spaghetti; overcooked it becomes flabby, undercooked it is tough and rubbery. There are several different textures to the tripe, the honeycomb probably being the best bit, but it is a good idea to mix it with some of the other pieces.

Always wash tripe well before cooking and dry it carefully, as it holds a lot of water which can spoil a rich sauce.

Tripe is so cheap compared with most other kinds of meat that you can afford to be a bit extravagant with its dressing up; so if the recipe demands a glass of wine and a dash of brandy, don't hold back, it is worth it.

Put the well-washed tripe, in a piece, with the sliced onions, into a flame-proof casserole or large lidded saucepan with the seasoning, bayleaf and mace and the ham, pork or bacon rinds. Just cover with water and milk, season, bring to the boil, cover the pan and simmer gently for 45 minutes. Fish out the onions with a slotted spoon, and if the tripe is not yet tender, let it go on cooking. Sieve the onions, and strain the cooked tripe. Make a pint of Béchamel with the flour, butter and some of the strained liquid from the tripe, add the onion purée and season well. Cut the drained tripe into strips or small squares, smother it with the sauce, in the casserole in which it cooked. Reheat in the oven and serve very hot with triangles of bread fried golden in a mixture of oil and butter, or pork dripping.

☐ *This is a very traditional English way of cooking tripe.*

Very often people don't really enjoy tripe until they have eaten it two or three times, but once acquired the taste is there for good, and those who do appreciate it, appreciate it very much; there is something deeply soothing about the flavour.

For 4

Italian Tripe

2 lbs prepared tripe, half cooked (see page 121),
  washed and dried
1 tablespoon olive oil
4 oz salt pork belly, cut in small chunks
1 onion, 1 clove garlic, chopped
large glass white wine
2–3 tomatoes, skinned and chopped
1 tablespoon tomato purée
salt and freshly ground pepper
bouquet of bayleaf, parsley, rosemary and thyme
4 tablespoons grated Parmesan
1 cup fresh breadcrumbs, fried golden in butter

Heat the olive oil in a flameproof dish, deep enough
to cook in, but shallow enough to go under the grill.
Brown the onion and salt pork slowly. Add the
tripe cut in one-inch squares, and the garlic and
white wine and simmer, uncovered, until the liquid is
reduced by half — after about 15 minutes. Add the
tomatoes, tomato purée, herbs and seasoning, cover
the pan and simmer until the tripe is just tender,
about 30–45 minutes. The sauce should be fairly
thick, but add a little water if it starts to stick at
the bottom. Preheat the grill. When ready, remove
the herbs, stir in three tablespoons of Parmesan,
strew the top with the breadcrumbs and the remaining Parmesan, and grill until piping hot all
through and lightly browned on top.

For 4

Portuguese Tripe

1½ lbs prepared tripe, carefully washed and dried
1 onion, sliced into rings
4 tablespoons olive oil
1 tablespoon flour
1 lb tomatoes, skinned and chopped
2 cloves garlic, crushed
few sprigs parsley
sprinkling dried marjoram
salt and freshly ground pepper
2–3 green chilli peppers, cut in strips, seeds removed
dash of white wine

Fry the onions in the oil, in a flameproof casserole,
until the rings have separated and become transparent. Add the tripe, cut in small pieces, and brown
lightly. Cook it rather fast at this stage or the tripe
will get very juicy and won't brown. Add the flour,
tomatoes, garlic, herbs, salt and pepper, chillies
and wine, and simmer covered in a slow oven, Reg
1½/290°, for one hour. This is a very good rich moist
stew with a hot flavour; it comes originally from
Portugal, via Dahomey, but has been considerably
modified. If you use bottled chillies, use six or
seven as they are milder than fresh ones.

For 4

Ox-Tongue

1 ox-tongue, salted and if possible smoked, of about
 3 lbs (Sainsbury's have these often)
3 carrots
3 onions
1 stick celery
1 fresh pig's trotter (if salted, soak with the tongue)
parsley, thyme, bayleaf
peppercorns
mustard sauce (page 181)

Soak the tongue for 24 hours changing the water
once or twice. Put it in a large casserole with the
sliced vegetables, add the pig's foot and enough
water to cover. Throw in the peppercorns and the
bunch of herbs, bring gently to the boil and simmer
in the oven in a covered casserole at Reg 2/300°
for $3\frac{1}{2}$–$4\frac{1}{2}$ hours. Take out of the liquid and skin
while the tongue is still very hot. Put it on a dish
and serve hot with mustard sauce.

If you want it cold, strain and reduce the liquid in
which it cooked to about one third, so it will set to a
firm jelly when cold. Taste it for salt; if it is too
salty you must dilute it and add aspic. Some cooks
prefer to lay the tongue out on a plate, top side up,
and glaze with the almost-set jelly, but you can roll
it up, squeeze it into a straight-sided round dish, fill
the spaces with the reduced cooking liquid,
press with a weighted plate for 24 hours, and turn
it out before serving. Some people think it looks
prettier like this in a jellied shape, and that laid out
on a dish it looks as though it will say 'ouch' when
you cut it.

For 6

Calves' Tongues with Salt Pork

$\frac{3}{4}$ lb salt pork belly (lean end, not soaked)
4 calves' tongues
1 onion
1 stick celery
2 carrots
sprigs parsley
peppercorns

Put the cleaned chopped vegetables in a large
saucepan with the parsley and peppercorns, tongues
and freshly salted pork, rind removed. Just cover
with water, bring to the boil and simmer really
slowly for $2\frac{1}{4}$–$2\frac{1}{2}$ hours, with the water just moving
gently. The salt from the pork is absorbed by the
tongues as they cook.

When they are tender take them out and skin them,
as soon as they are cool enough, starting underneath
the tips and removing the skin from front to back
in large pieces. Remove any bones, trim them, and
put into a hot dish with the salt pork, removed
from the bone and cut into large cubes (about two
inches across). Sprinkle with chopped parsley and
serve very hot with parsley sauce or mustard sauce
(page 181) and plain boiled potatoes.

☐ *This recipe came from the butcher. The calves'
tongues become an appetising pink from the salt in the
pork. Sheeps' tongues can also be cooked this way.*

For 4

Brains

Brains in Batter

2 calves' or 3 sheep's brains
flour for dusting
fritter batter (page 60)
salt and freshly ground pepper
oil or fat for deep frying
tomato sauce (page 185)

The Preparation of Brains

Calves' brains are the best; you need one set per person. Lambs' brains are much smaller, so buy three sets for two people. Soak the brains in tepid water for half an hour or more. Remove the skin and membranes and all the red threads. Blanch in simmering salted water, acidulated with lemon juice, for fifteen minutes or more. If they still seem too slippery and fragile to handle you can firm them up by chilling in the refrigerator for an hour or so, or even freezing in the ice-compartment before slicing or cooking them in batter etc.

Heat the oil or fat in a deep-frying pan. Prepare the brains as described. Cut the brains into halves or, if you prefer, into four. Dry, and dust with seasoned flour. Using a spoon, coat the brains with batter and fry carefully to a golden brown. Serve with tomato sauce.

For 2

Brains in White Sauce

4 lambs' or 2 calves' brains
2 oz butter
1 oz flour
¼ pint milk, infused with a sliced onion, 8 peppercorns
    and a bayleaf
good pinch nutmeg
salt and freshly ground pepper
juice of ½ lemon

Prepare the brains as on page 124. They should be
perfectly white. Remove the stem and slice each
brain in half. Make a well flavoured sauce with half
the butter, the flour and the milk, seasoned with
nutmeg, salt and freshly ground pepper. Melt the
remaining ounce of butter in a frying pan and gently
fry the brains for three or four minutes, seasoning
with salt and pepper. Add the sauce to the brains,
simmer four minutes more, stirring very carefully.
Transfer it carefully to a heated serving dish,
sprinkle with lemon juice and serve.

For 4

Pigs' Kidneys with Lovage

2 pigs' kidneys
salt and freshly ground pepper
pork dripping, or oil and butter
juice of ½ lemon
1 tablespoon lovage, finely chopped, or celery leaves
    or celery salt

About half an hour before you will eat them, slice
the kidneys finely, removing all the fatty core, and
sprinkle with salt and pepper. Leave for 25 minutes.
Melt the fat, or oil and butter, in a thick frying pan,
so that the bottom is liberally covered. Raise the
heat and fry the kidney slices briskly, a few at a
time, so that each slice gets an even contact with
the heat. As soon as both sides have changed colour
from dark red to pale brown, put the pieces in a
heated serving dish.

Finish by sprinkling with lemon juice and chopped
lovage. Serve at once with their own juices and
mashed potato.

☐ *Lovage, once you have it, is very easy to grow and
is perennial like mint. It is similar in flavour to raw
celery leaves; if you haven't any lovage use celery
instead.*

For 2

Kebabs with Lambs' Kidneys

4 lambs' kidneys
4 rashers bacon, rinds removed
1 large onion
6 firm tomatoes
1 pimento, seeds removed
12 small mushrooms
12 basil leaves
juice of ½ lemon
olive oil
salt and freshly ground pepper
two bayleaves
thyme

Skin, core and slice each kidney into four. Cut the bacon into one-inch squares. Quarter the onions and part the pieces, halve the tomatoes, cut the pimento into one-inch squares, remove the mushroom stalks. Put the meat and vegetables, including the basil leaves, in a bowl, and sprinkle with lemon juice, plenty of olive oil, salt, pepper and thyme. Add the bayleaves and marinate for about half an hour. Divide everything between eight skewers, alternating the ingredients and putting the basil leaves against the cut side of the tomatoes. Grill or barbecue, brushing with more oil, turning frequently. They take five or ten minutes. Serve with plain rice and a green salad. Mix the left-over marinade (and the juices from the grill-pan if you are indoors) into the rice before serving.

For 4

Kidneys with Lemon Juice

4 lambs' kidneys, skinned and cored
3 cloves garlic
juice of ½ lemon
dash white wine
salt and freshly ground pepper
sprig parsley, chopped
oil for frying

Chop the kidneys into pieces about ¾ inch thick. Heat a heavy frying pan until it is very very hot. Chop the garlic and when the pan is ready pour in a little oil, just enough to cover the bottom, and throw in the garlic. To this add the kidneys and sauté them three or four minutes, moving and turning them with a wooden spoon or fork all the time. Add the lemon juice, wine, chopped parsley and seasoning. Let it sizzle up and serve immediately with rice.

For 2

Kidney Pilaff

4–5 lambs' kidneys
1 onion, sliced
1 tablespoon olive oil
1 tablespoon butter
2 bayleaves
sprig of thyme
2 tablespoons tomato purée, moistened with a little
  stock
salt and freshly ground pepper
1 dessertspoon wine vinegar

Sauté the onion in oil and butter, in a sauté pan, without browning. Skin and core the kidneys and chop them into thin slices across. Sauté with the onions, bayleaves and thyme, for five to six minutes. Add the tomato purée and stock, and the vinegar, salt and pepper. Stir in and heat through. Serve with plain rice.

For 2

Rognon de Boeuf Saignant

1 ox kidney
2½ oz unsalted butter
small bunch parsley
salt and freshly ground pepper

Cut the kidney into half-inch slices, removing all the fatty core. Chop the parsley.
Heat one ounce of the butter in a heavy frying pan. When it is really hot, with a blue haze rising, put in the slices of kidney. Sauté for two or three minutes, moving them around in the pan. Turn them over and cook the other side in the same way. Meanwhile melt the rest of the butter in a small pan with the chopped parsley, without letting it brown. When the slices of kidney are browned on both sides, put them in a heated dish, throwing out the butter in which they cooked. Pour the freshly melted butter and parsley over, sprinkle with salt and freshly ground pepper and serve immediately. They will be very pink inside and very tasty; the red juice which they make mingles well with the butter. Serve with watercress and puréed potatoes.

For 4

Grilled Liver on a Skewer

¾ lb liver, lambs' or calves', sliced thickly
1 onion
1 red or green pimento
2 tablespoons olive oil
juice of ½ lemon
thyme
salt and freshly ground pepper

Prepare one hour before you start to cook. Cut the liver into squares about ¾ inch across. Cut the onions and pimentoes into pieces about the same size. Mix the olive oil and lemon juice, salt, pepper and thyme. Marinate the liver, peppers and onions in this for an hour.

Take out the pieces of meat and vegetables and put them on skewers, alternating meat, onion and pepper. Grill under a fairly fast heat, turning from time to time. Serve with plain boiled rice, to which you can add the juices from the grill pan.

For 2–3

Liver Provençale

1 lb lambs' liver, cut in thin slices
olive oil
2 cloves garlic
small bunch parsley
flour
butter
wine vinegar
salt and freshly ground pepper

Chop the garlic and parsley finely. Pat a little flour, seasoned with salt and pepper, into the liver to absorb the moisture. Heat half a tablespoon of oil in a really heavy frying pan. Meanwhile in a saucepan melt a good dollop of butter, without browning, and add the chopped garlic and parsley.

When the oil is really hot, with a blue haze rising, put in the slices of liver, flip them over and remove them to a hot dish. They should not have more than one or two minutes' cooking altogether. Take the frying pan off the heat and add the butter and garlic mixture. Add a dash of vinegar, let it sizzle up and pour it, still sizzling, over the liver.

Serve immediately with a purée of potatoes or turnips.

For 4

Sweetbreads

Fricasseed Sweetbreads

1 lb poached sweetbreads, kept warm
1 pint of stock in which they were poached (see
   opposite)
1 oz butter
1 oz flour
juice of 1 lemon
2 egg yolks
salt and freshly ground pepper
parsley, chopped
½ lb mushrooms (optional)

The preparation of sweetbreads

This preparation applies whatever the recipe, and to both lambs' and calves' sweetbreads.

Wash under a running tap, or soak in frequently changed salted water for one to three hours, until they are no longer pink but pearly white. Put into a pan of cold, salted water and bring slowly to the boil; boil two or three minutes, remove and cool at once in cold water. This stiffens them, making them easier to handle. Skin and remove all the lumps of gristle you can. Press between two plates for an hour.

The main methods of cooking from this point are: Poaching — poach in stock until tender, then use in a fricassée. Frying — (1) slice the sweetbreads; flour, egg-and-crumb and fry gently. Serve with tomato sauce (page 185); (2) slice, dip in fritter batter and fry gently; (3) slice and sauté quite simply in butter, for 10–15 minutes. After they are cooked, make a quick sauce in the pan with cream and a few mushrooms previously sautéed in butter, or serve them plain, sprinkled with lemon juice.

Strain one pint of the stock in which the sweetbreads were poached and make a sauce with the flour and butter and strained liquid. Mix the lemon juice with the egg yolks, season with salt and pepper and add to the sauce, away from the heat, stirring attentively; once it is mixed in, the sauce can no longer curdle. Let it thicken, then pour the sauce over the sliced sweetbreads and sprinkle with parsley. Serve with boiled or mashed potatoes.

You can add ½ lb mushrooms, first cooked in the stock, to the sauce.

For 4

Sausage Meat

¾ lb cheap cut of pork
¼ lb pork fat
2 thickish slices bread (about 3 oz)
grated rind lemon
pinch nutmeg
2 teaspoons salt
1 teaspoon freshly ground pepper
parsley, sage and thyme, finely chopped, according
    to taste and availability
touch of garlic if liked

Trim the meat of sinews and gristle. Soak the bread
in water, squeeze dry and crumble into a large bowl.
Mince the meat once, then add the fat and mince
again, not too finely. Put into the bowl with the
bread and add the lemon peel, herbs, spices and
seasoning. Mix thoroughly with your hands. If
you can get sausage skins, rinse them through
under the cold tap, and then fill them. If you haven't
an electric mincer with a sausage-filling attach-
ment, run the skin on to a large funnel and push the
meat through with the handle of a wooden spoon.
Twist at intervals to make separate sausages. If
you cannot buy sausage skins, use caul fat, which
should be soaked before use in salted water and then
cut into four-inch squares in which you enfold a
tablespoon of your sausage meat. Or you can make
skinless sausages rolled in flour.

☐ *It makes about 16 medium sausages.*

Sausages with White Wine Sauce

1½ lbs spicy French or Italian sausages
glass white wine
1½ oz butter
scant 1 oz flour
½ pint milk (infused with onion, bayleaf and
    peppercorns)
salt and freshly ground pepper
mashed potatoes *or* cooked haricot beans

Make half a pint of Béchamel with one ounce of
butter, and the flour and milk. Season with salt and
pepper. Soak the sausages in lukewarm water for a
few minutes. This helps to prevent them from burst-
ing. Dry them, prick all over and fry gently in the
remaining half ounce of butter until practically
done, pouring the fat off from time to time. Add the
wine, and when it is reduced by half, take out the
sausages and keep hot, or arrange them on a moun-
tain of mashed potatoes, or plain, cooked haricot
beans. Add the Béchamel to the wine in the frying
pan, stir it well and pour over the sausages. This
sauce is a good addition to bangers and mash, but
the bangers need to be a bit special to be worth it.

For 4

Toad in the Hole

6 large sausages
6 slices streaky bacon
for the batter:
4 oz plain flour
salt
2 eggs
½ pint milk
2–3 tablespoons oil or good pork dripping

Make a pudding batter by sieving the flour and salt into a bowl, make a well in the centre and add the eggs, breaking the yolks with your spoon before you start stirring. Add the milk gradually, stirring in the flour little by little until half the milk is added; keep going until all the flour is taken up and the mixture is smooth. Then add the rest of the milk and beat for five or ten minutes. Stand the batter in a cool place for one hour. Preheat oven to Reg 9/475°. When batter is ready, skin the sausages, heat the oil or dripping in a baking tin, fry the bacon two or three minutes, then add the skinned halved sausages. Put the tin in the oven for five minutes, then pour on the batter and cook for five minutes at Reg 9/475° and 35–40 minutes at Reg 7/425°.

For 4

Sausage with Lentils

1 cotechino or poaching sausage, of ¾–1 lb (available from delicatessen shops)
¾ lb small green lentils
2 cloves garlic
1 stick celery, chopped
butter
salt

Soak the lentils for three or four hours, then wash them and place in a pan of cold water with the peeled cloves of garlic and stick of celery. Bring slowly to the boil, skim and simmer gently for 1–1½ hours, adding salt half-way through, when they have started to get tender. Three-quarters of an hour before you want it ready, put the sausage, pricked all over with a needle, into a pan of cold water. Bring it gradually to the boil and poach in slowly simmering water for three-quarters of an hour.

Strain the lentils, keeping the liquid for soup, and add a large nut of butter. Serve with the sausage cut in slices and a good glass of rough red wine.

For 4

Stuffed Vine Leaves

20–30 vine leaves, fresh, or bought ready for use at
   Greek or Cypriot shops
3 oz rice (6 oz cooked rice)
4 oz minced lamb, beef or pork, raw or cooked
1 small onion
pinch ground coriander (or fresh leaves)
pinch ground cumin
salt and freshly ground pepper
good squeeze of lemon
¼–½ pint stock or tomato juice
olive oil

If you have fresh vine leaves, trim off the stalks and
plunge them into boiling salted water for five minutes.
Drain and let them cool while you fry the onion,
finely chopped, in oil until it is quite brown. Boil
the rice, unless you have some ready cooked. Brown
the meat with the onions if you are using fresh meat;
if using cold cooked meat, chop it finely. Mix the
onion, meat, rice and spices, and add salt and
pepper to taste. Put a teaspoon of the mixture on the
rough side of each leaf, wrap neatly into a little
parcel, lay them side by side in a flat flameproof
dish (they don't need tying), squeeze lemon juice
over and pour on the stock or tomato juice. Cover
with a plate that fits right down on to the vine
leaves, to stop them coming apart. Cook over a very
low heat for half an hour. Serve cold.

☐ *These are good served with drinks before dinner,
especially if you have your own vine, and can make them
quite small, choosing leaves that make good wrappers
— not too indented, and not too old and tough.*

Makes 20–30

Chicken Livers with Sage

1 lb chicken livers, cut in pieces
1 oz butter
2 slices bacon, rinds removed, cut in pieces
salt and freshly ground pepper
3 or 4 fresh sage leaves, chopped, or 1 teaspoon
   dried sage
sherry

Melt the butter in a small iron pan, and sauté the
pieces of bacon for a minute or two. Add the chicken
livers, a little salt, pepper and sage and cook five
minutes, stirring them about a bit. Remove the
chicken livers and bacon to a hot dish and keep
them warm, while you add a dash of sherry and a
similar amount of water to the pan, and let it
sizzle for a minute, stirring to release the sediment.
Pour the juices over the livers and serve with
Risotto Milanese (page 167) or plain boiled rice.

For 4

POULTRY AND GAME

Poultry and Game

It really is worth buying boiling chickens; it may seem more difficult because of the time factor, but, thinking ahead, you can put a nice fat hen in a pot with some herbs and vegetables, cover it with water and put it to simmer very gently while you go out. It can sit there for hours, gradually becoming tender, and it makes large amounts of delicious broth. It is worth going further to find a bird that has had a happy life, but even a battery hen has a remote resemblance to chicken, once carefully cooked. All poultry is now fairly cheap, since it is reared on such a vast scale.

When you buy a fresh chicken, don't forget to take home the giblets (and if you buy a frozen one don't forget to look inside before you cook it, as polythene does not make a good stuffing); the giblets are invaluable for gravy or stock or to improve the flavour of the sauce that goes with the chicken, and the liver is a good addition to most stuffings.

Game, both for casseroling and roasting, is getting scarcer and more expensive every year, but still seems to be cheaper in the country. It is worth remembering that the birds are only young and plump at the beginning of the season, and become increasingly thin and tough as the winter wears on. Young pigeons are available only from March to October, and even in those months make certain you have not got dad or grandad from the year before. The same applies to wild bunnies, though tame rabbits are not allowed to go on hopping about long enough to get tough.

Full instructions are given for the drawing, plucking and trussing of birds, and the drawing and skinning of rabbits or hares, for anyone lucky enough to get a present of game, but a pheasant run into by a car is unlikely to make good eating, poor thing, because of the bruises.

To Pluck and Draw and Truss a Bird

Plucking

As with rabbits and hares, game-birds from friends tend to arrive fully clad. In the case of most game, and depending on the weather, it should hang for a week to ten days before being plucked. Hang, head uppermost, in a cool airy place. Pigeons are eaten fresh, but can be kept hanging in their feathers for a few days until they are wanted.

The chief problem with plucking, for someone who hasn't done it before, is controlling the feathers, so choose a small room with an easily swept floor (on a still day it can be done out of doors). Sit down with the bird on a table in front of you and a large carrier bag or cardboard box at your feet or on your lap.

Hold the bird by one wing and start under the wings, pulling a few feathers at a time with a sharp pinching tug. Always pull in the direction they are pointing, not against the grain, or you may tear the skin. Carry on plucking from the wings and lower neck, steadily leaving the skin bare and working towards the tail. When you come to the big strong wing feathers pull them out one by one. Don't be tempted to cut them, as you will be left with awkward stumps. Drop each handful of feathers into the box or bag as you pull it out. A mound of pheasant feathers is a pretty sight, but one puff of air, even if it's only somebody laughing, and they are all over the place. There is no need to pluck the neck or head.

When you have finished, there will be a few tufts of down here and there, so light a twist of paper or a taper and turn the bird round a few inches above it to singe off every whisker that remains.

Drawing

Trussing

Lay the plucked bird breast down and feel for the place where the neck joins the shoulders. Cut through the skin about two inches above this point. Put your knife in under the skin and cut through the neck where it joins the shoulders. Draw out the neck, leaving a flap of skin for covering the hole. Carefully pull out the crop, without breaking it (it is a bag full of grit and grains), and the windpipe. Keep the neck for the giblet stock, and throw the head away. Put your finger into the hole between the shoulders and run it all round the inside of the bird, as if it was a knife loosening a pudding in a basin.

Turn the bird on its back and just under the tail you will find the vent Cut all round this, right through the skin. You can then pull this away and put your hand, or fingers if it is a small bird, right inside to pull out the loosened innards. Look for the gall bladder attached to the liver. It is oval, small, dark brown and full of very bitter yellow liquid. If this bursts it is the ruin of the bird, as the strong taste doesn't easily wash away, so cut away the gall bladder first. Cut out the gizzard (a hard, dark reddish object) and slice it almost through, but stop at the grey skin, which is a bag with more undesirable contents. Throw this away but keep the healthy reddish outside part, plus the liver and heart. Throw everything else away, and wash and wipe the inside of the bird.

The neck, liver, heart and gizzard make giblet gravy. Cut off the bird's feet, pulling out the tough tendons from feet to thighs as you do so, if possible.

This method does not use skewers.

(A) Lay the drawn bird on its back with its tail towards you and make the cuts shown in the diagram; tuck the front flap of skin at its neck over the neck hole and down over the back. Flip the pinions (the last joint of the wing) inwards and tuck them behind the shoulders.

(B) Take about 3 feet of string and pass it under the bird's shoulders, the loose ends being one in each hand on each side of the bird.

(C) Pull the string up under the wings of the bird, over the shoulders, down the back of each wing, past the elbows, past the legs. Pull it up under the thigh joints and, without letting go, pull it all tight, and flip the bird over onto its front. Tie a knot in the middle of the back, and turn it over again.

(D) The bird should now be looking much neater, plumped up with its legs drawn up to its wings. Bring the two ends of the string down the back and knot them over the parson's nose.

If you want to stuff the bird, do it now.

(E) Bring the ends of the string from the knot on the parson's nose and tie the drumsticks firmly together, below the breastbone.

A

B

C

D

E

Boning a Chicken or Duck

Find a knife with a short thin blade and sharpen it extra well. Turn the drawn chicken over and cut along the middle of its back from neck to tail (1). Sliding your knife hard up against the carcass of the bird, work your way round one side, slowly pulling the meat away with your fingers to expose the line for your next cut (2). When you encounter the leg, feel with your free forefinger for the ball and socket joint and slide the point of your knife into it to free it. Continue cutting round, disengaging the wing, but cutting outside the fine flat bone that lies beneath it on the carcass. When you have cut round to the flat side of the breastbone, start on the other side of the back in the same way. Cut the skin from the ridge of the breastbone very carefully indeed as it is paper-thin here. Lift out the carcass, leaving the parson's nose on it. You can remove the upper leg and wing bones (3) by sliding your fingers and knife down close to the bone and cutting firmly through the joint. Remove the wing tips completely, skin, bone and all, or you can leave the last two wing bones and the drumsticks (shown as dotted outlines) where they are. The flesh can now be flattened out, skin side down, seasoned and sprinkled with wine, and any rich stuffing put in the centre (4). The bird is wrapped round this and made more or less into a chicken shape again, and the opening tied, skewered or sewn together (5). You can roast this stuffed chicken or simmer it in stock.

A pâté mixture of pork and veal with perhaps a few pistachio nuts and a good proportion of fat makes an excellent stuffing. Serve it cold, with the threads removed and the seam-side down. Cut it right across in slices like any pâté. You can bone a duck in exactly the same way. If you sew the opening rather than tying it, the bird miraculously goes back into shape while it is cooking.

1

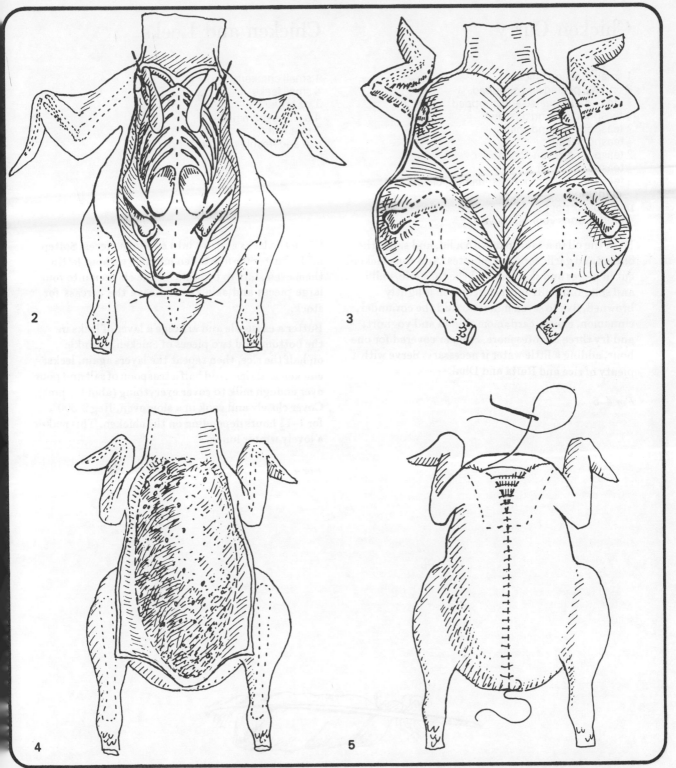

Chicken Curry

1 small roasting chicken
3 onions, peeled and chopped
1 clove garlic peeled and chopped
½ teaspoon ground turmeric
½ teaspoon ground chilli
½ teaspoon salt
2 teaspoons ground coriander
½ teaspoon cumin
¼ teaspoon each ground cinnamon, cloves and
    cardamom
pinch black pepper
4 tablespoons yoghurt, olive oil

Heat the oil in a saucepan with a lid, and sauté the
onions and garlic for a few minutes. Add the chicken,
cut in pieces and skinned, and the turmeric, chilli
and salt, and sauté until the chicken is lightly
browned, five to seven minutes. Add the coriander,
cinnamon, cloves, cardamom, cumin and yoghurt,
and fry three minutes more. Simmer covered for one
hour, adding a little water if necessary. Serve with
plenty of rice and Raïta and Dhal.

For 4–5

Chicken and Leeks

1 small chicken
4 small leeks
1 oz butter
4 oz long grain rice
1 pint milk
salt and freshly ground pepper

Clean the leeks and cut into one-inch pieces. Soften
in the butter for five to ten minutes without letting
them even start to brown. Cut the chicken into four
large pieces and skin them. Leave the carcass for
stock.

Butter a casserole and arrange a layer of leeks in
the bottom, add two pieces of chicken, sprinkle
on half the rice, then repeat the layers again, leeks,
chicken and rice. Add half a teaspoon of salt and pour
over enough milk to cover everything (about a pint).
Cover closely and cook in a slow oven, Reg 2/300°,
for 1–1½ hours depending on the chicken. This makes
a lovely winter lunch.

For 4

Chicken Pie

1 small boiling chicken
2 carrots, 1 onion
8 peppercorns, 1 bayleaf, salt
1 oz butter, 1 oz flour
juice of ½ lemon
chopped parsley
6 rashers bacon
4 oz mushrooms
plain pie pastry (page 218)
top of the milk

Cover the chicken with water in a large saucepan, bring slowly to the boil, skim and add the sliced vegetables, bayleaf, peppercorns and salt. Simmer for 1½ hours or longer, until the bird is tender. Allow to cool a little in the cooking liquid. Preheat oven to Reg 7/425°. Make a sauce with the butter, flour and ¾ pint of the strained, hot chicken broth. Throw in the mushrooms whole and simmer for eight minutes. Check for seasoning. Skin the chicken and cut it into pieces. Roll the bacon rashers, rinds removed, and keep together with toothpicks while you fry them gently for 15 minutes. Remove the toothpicks.

Mix the chicken pieces, chopped parsley and lemon juice into two thirds of the mushroom sauce, keeping the remaining sauce aside, and turn the mixture into a pie dish. Lay the bacon rolls on top and cover with pastry. Brush with top of the milk and bake at Reg 7/425° for ten minutes and then at Reg 4/350° for 20 minutes or longer. Serve with the extra sauce.

☐ *A bright green vegetable such as sprouts, broccoli, or best of all fresh peas, sets off the pale interior of the pie. It is also delicious eaten cold.*

For 4–6

Chicken Paprika

An elderly chicken, jointed in small pieces
2–3 onions, chopped
2 tablespoons oil and butter, or chicken fat
2 tablespoons paprika
¼ pint sour cream
salt to taste

Brown the pieces of chicken in oil and butter or chicken fat, in a flameproof casserole, remove them to a dish and fry the onions in the same fat. Stir in the paprika, let it cook for a minute, then return the chicken, season and cover very tightly with foil and the pan lid. Leave to simmer very slowly or put in a low oven, Reg 2½/315°, for 1–1½ hours, depending on the age of the chicken. When it is tender, thicken the copious juice with half the sour cream just before serving (don't let it boil).

Serve each helping with an extra dollop of sour cream and a sprinkling of paprika on top. Boiled noodles tossed in butter are lovely with this dish.

For 4

To Skin A Rabbit or Hare

If you have never skinned a rabbit or hare the sight of one of these otherwise welcome gifts on the kitchen table, with fur intact, is rather upsetting. It must be skinned before it can be cooked, and this is really (once you've done it four or five times) quite easy and not too awful. If you can't face it you will have to take the whole thing to a butcher, but think of the time saved if you can do it yourself. A hare should be well hung (head down) but a rabbit should be gutted as soon as possible. Lay the animal on several layers of newspaper. Take a sharp pointed knife, find the lower tip of the breast bone and slit the skin right through. Make an incision from the tip of the breastbone to the base of the tail. This can be done without looking the first time, if your sense of direction is accurate. Do be sure you have gone through the skin, or you will have to do it again to extract the innards. Having made this incision pick up the animal, front legs in one hand, back legs in the other, belly to the newspaper, and shake; the intestines will drop on to the paper. Boldly pull any that remain, until you find you are dealing with relatively familiar pieces like liver and kidneys; take these out and put them aside. Throw the intestines away. Then get on with the skinning. Starting with the original incision, peel the skin away towards the spine on each side. Flip the back legs inside out, as if you were taking off very difficult stockings. Sever the legs at the heel joint (the bend above the foot) and cut off the tail. The back and the middle of the animal should now be skinned.

Pull the skin up towards the head, flipping out the front legs as you did the back, and severing the legs at the first joint above the foot; go on pulling the skin towards the head. The easy way out is not to skin the head, but to chop it off as soon as the neck is clear. However, if you feel you need the head, which makes good stock, you must carefully cut round the ears and eyes, and pull the whole skin over the head, ending at the mouth.

With the rabbit or hare now naked, make an incision between the back legs and clean it well under a running tap. Break the membrane across the rib cage, take out the heart and lungs and wash it all very well. Before cooking a rabbit, it is a good idea to get rid of the slime left after skinning, and also the sour grass taste of a wild rabbit, by soaking in fairly heavily salted water for an hour. This also helps to whiten the flesh. A hare will need a good rinsing, as it always seems to be so much bloodier than a rabbit.

Jointing is fairly simple. The back legs are severed where they join the backbone, and then divided along the centre of the pelvis. The next piece (the saddle) continues till the ribs begin. The ribs have the front legs and shoulder joined on, and again can be split down the centre. The head is not used except for making stock. The kidneys can be left in the saddle, but the liver should be kept aside, as it helps to make a good sauce. The heart can be left under the ribs, or used with the head for stock.

Rabbit Stew

1 small rabbit
6 oz fresh belly of pork
1 onion, finely chopped
butter and oil for frying
1 glass white wine
1½ lbs tomatoes, peeled and chopped
1 bunch parsley, tied with thread
1 clove garlic, chopped
salt and freshly ground pepper
parsley and garlic to finish

Remove the rind and cut the pork into cubes; sizzle it in the oil and butter in a sauté pan until the fat begins to run. Add the onion and soften it, browning only slightly. Add the jointed rabbit and brown the pieces thoroughly. Bring the wine to the boil in a small pan. Pour it over the rabbit and add the tomatoes, parsley, garlic, salt and pepper. Turn the heat down and simmer uncovered, stirring from time to time and turning the pieces of rabbit, for 1–1½ hours until the rabbit is tender.

Serve in a gratin dish, spooning the pork and tomatoes over the rabbit and sprinkle with freshly chopped parsley and garlic.

For 4

Sauté of Rabbit with Mustard

1 tender young rabbit, jointed, and its liver
butter and oil for frying
2 shallots, sliced into rings
2 rashers bacon, rinds removed, cut in pieces
1 glass white wine
generous sprig thyme
salt and freshly ground pepper
parsley, chopped
coffee cup thin cream, or top of the milk
2 teaspoons Dijon mustard

Melt enough butter and oil in a large shallow frying pan or casserole to cover the base of the pan. Fry the shallots for a minute, add the bacon, then turn up the heat and brown the rabbit pieces, keeping the liver aside. Add the wine and let it bubble a little, turn down the heat, add the thyme, salt and pepper, and let the rabbit cook, covered, until it is tender, which should be within half an hour or even less if it is a really young one. Remove the sprig of thyme.

Fry the liver separately in butter, chop or slice it and mix it with the cream and mustard. Pour this over the rabbit pieces, heat through, reduce by boiling if necessary, and serve sprinkled with parsley.

If you have a tough or large rabbit, cook it much longer. Flour the pieces before frying, and after the wine has bubbled up add half a pint of warm stock, which can be made from the head and giblets of the rabbit. Simmer until tender and then proceed as before to finish the sauce. If the sauce is not thick enough, add an egg yolk or beurre manié (page 220), or reduce by boiling rapidly.

Rabbit Escalopes

2 fillets from either side of the backbone of a large,
    tender rabbit
seasoned flour
1 egg, beaten
fine dried breadcrumbs
1 tablespoon each of butter and oil
butter
dash of sherry

Ask the butcher to take the fillets from the rabbit
before he joints it. If he refuses, take it home whole,
and with a sharp, pointed knife cut a line as near
the spine as you can, all along the back. Keep the
knife against the bone and carefully remove the
fillet. The underbelly, which is thin and flappy, will
come too; cut this off. Turn the fillets underside up,
so the silvery side is below, and cut lengthwise
almost through but not quite. Lay them on a piece
of well-oiled greaseproof paper, cover with another
piece and then bash, with either a proper steak
beater or a rolling pin. They will flatten out considerably to a neat pear shape.

Take them out of the paper, dip in seasoned flour,
then beaten egg, then crumbs. Fry gently in butter
and oil for about five minutes each side.

Remove them to a warm plate while you drop
another tablespoon of butter into the pan, raise
the heat, and as it froths add a dash of sherry. Stir
it quickly and pour a little of this good gravy on
each escalope.

☐ *This is only feasible if you have a large rabbit.*
Use the rest for a pâté, stew, pie or jelly.

For 2

Roast Saddle of Hare

1 saddle of hare, preferably marinated for two days
    (opposite) as this makes it more tender and tasty
    and improves the flavour of the gravy
flour
4 rashers bacon
butter, beef dripping or pork fat
water
salt and freshly ground pepper
¼ pint single cream or top of the milk

Take the hare out of the marinade and wipe it dry.
Remove the silvery membrane over the back with a
sharp knife. Preheat the oven to Reg 7/425°. Melt
about half an ounce of butter in a frying pan. Dust
the saddle with flour, brown it on all sides in the
butter, take it out and wrap in bacon rashers. Roast
in butter for 20–30 minutes, basting often. Add
half a glass of water five minutes before it is cooked.
Take off the bacon and put the hare with the rashers
on a hot serving dish to keep warm.

Pour off some of the butter from the roasting tin,
or scoop it off with a metal spoon. Add a minute
sprinkling of flour to the juices in the tin; let it
bubble a moment and stir in the cream. Heat gently,
taste for seasoning, and pour the small amount of
thickish sauce over the saddle.

Carve in lengthwise strips parallel to the backbone
and serve with puréed potatoes or celeriac or hot
beetroot.

☐ *Some people include the back legs to stretch the*
saddle further.

For 2–3

Jugged Hare

1 hare, jointed and cut up
seasoned flour
2 tablespoons lard or dripping
1 large onion
4 carrots
1 stick celery
bunch of parsley and thyme
4 cloves
8 peppercorns
stock, salt
1 tablespoon beurre manié (page 220)
small glass port, or 1 tablespoon redcurrant jelly

If you like, you can marinate the hare for 24 hours in the marinade for game (page 145). Wipe the joints dry and flour thoroughly all over. Heat the lard in a flameproof casserole and fry the joints quickly to brown them. Put them aside and put the sliced onion and the carrots and celery, cleaned and sliced, into the pan. Cover and allow to sweat for ten minutes. Replace the hare, add the herbs, cloves and peppercorns, and pour in enough stock just to cover. Add a little salt and simmer, covered, for one and a half hours, in the oven at Reg 2/300° or on top of the stove.

Remove the joints to a dish. Strain the liquid and reduce by almost half. Stir the beurre manié into the hare liquid making a smooth, thick sauce. Stir in the port or redcurrant jelly, put the hare back into the casserole or onto a nice white oval dish, and pour the sauce over.

Before serving allow it to stand in a hot place, without cooking, for ten minutes, to let the sauce and meat marry together again and the flavour develop.

☐ *If you have a large hare, keep the saddle to roast later (see opposite); if a small one, include it.*

For 4

Marinade for Game

¼ pint vinegar (wine or cider)
½ pint red wine
grating of nutmeg
bayleaf, sprig of thyme
2 large onions, finely sliced
salt and peppercorns

Mix everything together and pour it over the game in a china or glazed earthenware dish. Turn the meat over from time to time; you can leave it there from one to fourteen days.

Grilled Pigeon

one young pigeon per person (available from March
    to October)
salt, pepper and lemon juice
butter
dried breadcrumbs
Dijon mustard

Choose small pigeons in the hope that these are
young and therefore tender. Cut them through the
backbone, split them open and flatten them like
an open book. Season with salt and pepper and
sprinkle with lemon juice. Dot with butter, and
grill under medium heat, on the skin side first; turn
after 5–10 minutes, and spoon the other side with
the melted butter. Dab it with mustard and sprinkle
with breadcrumbs as soon as it is gently browned;
turn once more to the outside, dot with mustard,
baste with butter and sprinkle with more breadcrumbs; cook gently until slightly crisp and golden.
Serve with mustard sauce (page 181) and watercress.

Braised Pigeons with Celery Sauce

4 young pigeons
flour
2 heads celery
2 onions
2 oz bacon in a piece
butter
1 glass red wine
thyme, bayleaf
3 or 4 tablespoons cream
1 tablespoon beurre manié (page 220)
a little salt and plenty of freshly ground pepper

Cut the celery into half-inch pieces and chop the
onions coarsely. Cut the bacon into rough dice.
Heat the butter in a flameproof casserole, add the
bacon, and when it is sizzling brown the pigeons,
dusted in flour, in the fat for a few minutes, until
they are coloured on every side. Remove them to a
plate and put the vegetables into the casserole to
sweat, covered, for a few minutes. Lay the pigeons
on top and pour the heated wine over everything.
Add herbs, salt and pepper, cover and simmer on
top of the stove or in the oven at Reg 3/325°, so
that the liquid is almost, but not quite, boiling,
for about 1½ hours, or until the pigeons are tender.
Put the birds on a hot dish and keep warm with the
vegetables, scooped out of the sauce with a perforated spoon. Skim most of the fat off the juices
and thicken them with the beurre manié, stirring all
the time. The juice is copious, most of it coming
from the celery. Finish the sauce by stirring in the
cream, and taste for seasoning. Pour it over the
birds and vegetables and serve puréed potatoes.

☐ *An alternative method is to put a pint of fresh
shelled peas and a lettuce into the pot, instead of the
celery, about 25–30 minutes before the end of the
cooking.*

For 4

Vegetables

Vegetables

The only way to buy fresh vegetables, unless you want to pay the earth for them, is in season, and to buy them often so that they can be eaten absolutely fresh. There are dozens of different vegetables to be seen trundling in muddy lorries towards Covent Garden on any dark winter morning; parsnips, cabbages, sprouts, beetroots, carrots, endives, celeriac, swedes, celery, Jerusalem artichokes, red cabbage, turnips, winter spinach, onions, leeks, cauliflowers, spring greens and curly kale are all grown in Britain and are far, far cheaper to serve than the smallest handful of imported French beans. So, of course, are all the pulses that are so comforting on a cold day. Lettuces seem to struggle up all the year round, but they do become more expensive in winter and taste of less.

The best vegetables are home-grown, and at least home-grown herbs are a possibility for everyone, since they can be planted out quite happily in the smallest window-box. Parsley is almost always on sale, so it makes sense to concentrate on the more unusual herbs, tarragon, basil, lovage, even thyme, rosemary, sage and chives which can be made to feel at home on a city windowsill.

Since tomatoes are only in season for a few months (home-grown ones from August to October), it is worth remembering that tinned Italian tomatoes always make a good substitute in cooking. They are grown in blazing sunshine and have a beautiful sweet flavour even after they have been in a tin.

Most books on nutrition suggest peeling vegetables thinly, as many of the vitamins lie close to the surface and thick peeling disposes of too many of them; for economy this is important too, though it is not a rare sight to see even quite experienced cooks carving off the peel of potatoes, carrots, turnips, parsnips and so on in great chunks.

Nutrition books also suggest conservative (loaded word) cooking of green vegetables such as broccoli, cabbage, peas, beans and brussels sprouts. Their method is to use from half to one inch of water so the vegetables are virtually cooked in steam. But if you just cover them with salted water and cook them for the minimum time, they come out tasting and looking so much better and fresher that people are bound to eat more to make up for vitamins that have escaped. Once they are cooked, drained and smothered in butter they should be eaten straight away; they do not keep hot well, and lose their flavour and colour very fast.

With salads, there are two vital things that go wrong. One is that the salad is washed but not properly dried before the dressing goes on — the result, a soggy wasteland of tasteless wet green. Second, instead of being over-generous with oil and lubricating the salad to give it a wonderful unctuousness that contrasts with the crisp leaves, the vinegar (which should be wine or even cider but NEVER malt) is overdone and the result gives the palate a violent shock. Put the dressing on a green salad at the last possible minute, it goes listless so fast. A handful of sprigs of parsley, tarragon or chervil with stalks removed are a good addition to a green salad. Tomatoes aren't; make two separate salads instead of one jumbled one. Watercress makes a very good salad to accompany game or a juicy piece of beef, and is nearly always cheap.

Roast Jerusalem Artichokes

1½ lbs Jerusalem artichokes
lard or pork fat

Cook them like roast potatoes, parboiling for 2–5 minutes before putting into the hot fat. Baste them, put them in the oven and cook on the shelf below the meat, or put them in the roasting tin round the meat. They don't take as long as roast potatoes, about 30–40 minutes; they should be turned over carefully and basted once or twice.

☐ *Very good with roast pork. You can also cook parsnips like this.*

For 6

Aubergine Fritters

4 large aubergines
fritter batter (page 60)
salt
deep oil for frying

Cut the aubergines in lengthwise slices, sprinkle with salt, and allow them to drain for half an hour or more. Wash and dry the slices and coat them with batter. Heat the oil in a deep frying pan and deep-fry the aubergines to a golden brown. Drain very well before serving.

These are excellent with lamb.

☐ *This recipe is also fine for courgettes.*

For 6–8

Broad Beans in their own Sauce

2–4 lbs broad beans, depending on their age
½ oz butter
½ oz flour
top of the milk
1 tablespoon finely chopped parsley, chervil or
    savory
lemon juice
salt

Pod the beans. If they are young and tender include a section of the pod around some of them. If they are old and tough make sure you remove the crescent attached to the bean, and even their outer skin.

Bring salted water to the boil and throw them in. When tender, strain, keep the beans warm and reserve the liquid. In another pan melt the butter, make a white roux with the flour and gradually stir in a cup of the liquid, the top of the milk and the chopped herbs of your choice. When you have a smooth sauce add the beans and a squeeze of lemon, season with salt if necessary, and serve.

For 4

Broad Beans in Oil

1½ lbs broad beans, small and fresh
6 spring onions
3 tablespoons olive oil
½ lemon
salt and black pepper

Cut up the broad beans with their pods still on. Any that look tough or ropey should be shelled. Roughly chop the firm parts of the onions. Heat the oil in a thick saucepan, put in the beans and spring onions and sweat them very gently with the lid on for 10 or 15 minutes. Add the juice of half a lemon and half a cup of water, salt and pepper, and cook uncovered until soft, about an hour. If necessary add a little more water. They should be very tender with an intense flavour. Good hot or cold.

For 4

Chang's Cabbage

1½ lbs cabbage, green or white
2 tablespoons oil
few drops soy sauce
1 teaspoon salt
3 teaspoons sugar
2 tablespoons vinegar

Mix the salt, sugar and vinegar together. Slice the cabbage as finely as you can, discarding the tough stalks and outer leaves. Wash well and then shake as dry as possible in a cloth, as you would salad. Heat the oil in a large frying pan over a fairly high heat, and when it is really hot (but not burning), fling in the cabbage. Keep it moving about with a wooden fork, if you have one, or a spoon. As soon as it is all covered with oil, shake a few drops of soy sauce over it, then pour on the vinegar mixture. Let it cook a minute or two and serve at once, hot, crisp and juicy.

Children don't always like this, but adults like it as a change from universal plain boiled cabbage (though cabbage is not nearly as universal as it used to be, and boiled correctly it can be a really beautiful and delicious vegetable).

☐ *This is a sweet-sour cabbage, very Chinese but rather good with Shepherd's Pie or chops. It is also very quick — cooked in seconds.*

For 6

German Red Cabbage

1 medium-sized red cabbage
1–2 oz butter, 2 cloves garlic
1 large cooking apple, peeled and cut up
2 medium onions, peeled and sliced
bunch of thyme, parsley, and a bayleaf
grated orange rind or juice
1 teaspoon caraway seeds
pinch cinnamon, pinch nutmeg
salt and pepper
2 tablespoons brown sugar
small glass red wine (left-over is best as it becomes slightly vinegary)

Preheat oven to Reg 2/300°.

Take the large damaged outer leaves off the cabbage, quarter it and shred as finely as possible, discarding the centre core. Melt the butter in a flameproof casserole, add the cabbage and cook gently, covered, for five minutes. Add the apples, onions, garlic, a little grated orange rind, herbs, spices, salt and pepper. Mix everything together well, sprinkle on the sugar, add the wine, cover and put in the oven, for up to three hours. Check half-way through that it is not drying up, and if it is add a little hot water. This reheats very successfully, and is possibly even better for it.

☐ *A rich and filling dish.*

For 4–6

Red Cabbage Flamande

1 medium red cabbage
2 eating apples, peeled, quartered and cored
1 tablespoon caster sugar
2–3 tablespoons wine vinegar
salt, freshly ground pepper, and nutmeg
butter

Italian Carrots

1 lb carrots, old or young
1 oz butter
½ teaspoon salt
½ teaspoon sugar
1 dessertspoon flour
¼ pint water

Remove the outside leaves of the cabbage, cut it into quarters, cut out the stalk and slice the leaves into thin shreds. It shouldn't need washing. Put the sliced cabbage into a buttered casserole, with the apples, sprinkling the layers with the sugar, vinegar, salt, pepper and nutmeg. Cook, covered, at Reg 3/325° for 3–3½ hours. This mild, sweet dish of red cabbage is the perfect thing to serve with hare or any other game or with smoked boiling sausage, or frankfurters.

For 6

Cut the cleaned carrots into thin strips. Melt the butter in a thick saucepan with a close-fitting lid. Sweat the carrots gently in the butter for about five minutes. Add salt and sugar and sprinkle on the flour, mixing it well with a wooden spoon. Then gradually add the water, clamp down the lid tightly, and leave to simmer slowly for twenty minutes. The carrots will be very tasty and covered with a thick golden sauce.

☐ *This recipe is also perfect for tiny young turnips and for celery.*
If you cook celery in this way, blanch it first in boiling salted water for five minutes.

For 4

Carrottes Rapeés

1 large garden carrot for each person
6 tablespoons olive oil
1½ tablespoons white wine or cider vinegar
pinch of sugar, salt, and freshly ground pepper

Grate the carrots finely; make a dressing with the oil, vinegar, sugar, salt and pepper and turn the grated carrot in it until every shred is glistening.

In France they might serve this half and half with celeriac rémoulade (this page) or a salad of very finely shredded red cabbage tossed in a dressing heavily loaded with Dijon mustard.

For 5–6

Celeriac Rémoulade

2 heads celeriac
mayonnaise:
2 egg yolks
½ pint oil
vinegar (white wine or cider)
salt and freshly ground pepper
mustard powder

Make a very mustardy mayonnaise by combining a spoonful of the mayonnaise with at least a teaspoonful of mustard powder, and mixing it very well into the rest.

Peel the celeriac and cut it into thin strips or shred it on a mandoline. Mix in the mayonnaise quickly. It is quite common to blanch the shredded celeriac before adding the mayonnaise but this can make it soggy and spoil the flavour.

For 8

Courgettes in Butter

1½ lbs courgettes
2 oz butter
chopped parsley (or chervil, mint or chives)
salt and freshly ground pepper
lemon juice

Wash the courgettes and peel them if necessary.
Cut in half-inch rounds or quarter them lengthways,
then cut these slices in half.

Bring a pan of salted water to the boil and cook
the courgettes for five minutes. Drain well and return
to the rinsed and dried pan with the butter.
Sprinkle with whichever herb you choose and simmer
gently, without browning, until the courgettes are
tender, 10–15 minutes. Season, and add a squeeze of
lemon if you like.

For 4

Courgettes au Gratin

6 small courgettes
4 medium tomatoes, peeled and chopped
1 clove garlic
parsley, chopped
salt and freshly ground pepper
1 oz butter
2 tablespoons oil
½ cup dried breadcrumbs

Don't peel the courgettes unless they are elderly.
Slice into thick pennies and strew with salt, leaving
them in a colander or on a tilted plate for an hour or
so, to drain off some of their moisture.

Heat the oil and butter in a large frying pan, and toss
the dried courgettes, a few at a time, without
browning them. Keep them warm. Melt a little
more butter and oil and cook the chopped tomatoes,
garlic, salt, pepper and parsley, until you have
a thickened purée. Add the courgettes and turn the
mixture into a gratin dish. Cover with the breadcrumbs, dot with butter and cook in a hot oven,
Reg 7/425°, for half an hour.

For 4 (or 2 if served as a course on its own)

Chick Peas

Hummus with Tahina

½ lb chick peas, soaked overnight
¼ pint tahina paste (made of sesame seeds and
      bought in tins or bottles from Greek or Cypriot
      shops)
2 juicy lemons
2 cloves garlic, crushed
salt
olive oil

You cannot skimp the soaking of chick peas —
they must be soaked overnight. Wash them first,
then put them in a bowl large enough for them
almost to double in size. Cover well with water and
after their soaking cook them gently in the same water.
A pinch of bicarbonate of soda softens the water
and shortens the cooking time (rain water is, in fact,
the best thing to cook all pulses in). Add no salt
until the peas are almost tender. Cooking time
depends on the age of the peas: new, they can take
as little as half an hour, old, up to two hours.

The chick peas must be cooked very well (this page);
drain them and reserve their liquid. Greeks then roll
them with a rolling pin (in a large plastic bag) until
they are pulverised, which gives an uneven texture
but you can mouli or liquidise them, moistened with
a little of their liquid. When they are crushed, add
more of the cooking liquid, the tahina paste, lemon
juice, crushed garlic and salt. The taste must be
adjusted to the way you like it, some like more lemon,
some more garlic and so on. Serve, moistened with a
little more oil, on a plate, with a few spring onions
and some good hot bread. Eat this as a simple
lunch dish or a first course.

For 6

Crudités with Aïoli

6–8 carrots
2 green peppers
2 heads chicory
1 cucumber
6 sticks celery
6 tomatoes
2 heads fennel
aïoli (page 176)

This can be made with any fresh crisp vegetables.
Simply clean and cut them up, the carrots, peppers,
chicory, cucumber and celery into sticks about two
inches long, the tomatoes into quarters, the fennel
into slices.

Put the vegetables, each sort in a group, on a large
dish that just holds them all. Cover and chill
lightly; serve crisp and fresh with a powerful aïoli,
as the first course to an otherwise rich meal. Eat
them with your fingers, dipping each piece into a
dollop of aïoli on your plate.

For 6

Dandelion Salad

A handful of tender young dandelion leaves
chives, spring onions or mild onion, chopped
clove of garlic
2 tablespoons oil
1 teaspoon sugar
pinch of salt

Wash the leaves well and cut the stalks short.
Shake them dry, put them in a salad bowl and
sprinkle with chives, spring onion or mild onion.
Pulverise the garlic, add oil, sugar and salt and toss
into the salad. The dandelions are bitter, but if you
want a sharper taste, add a little lemon juice to the
dressing.

☐ *Ancient herb-lore says that if you select a healthy
young dandelion plant in the garden and lay a slate
or brick over it, the leaves will continue growing and
blanch themselves, which will make them more tender
and less bitter.*

For 2

Bulgour

½ lb coarsely ground wheat (from Greek or Health
  Food shops)
¼ lb Italian vermicelli
1 pint hot stock, bouillon or water
2–3 oz butter
salt
pepper
sprinkle of parsley

A deep, round earthenware dish with a lid is good
for cooking this in. Otherwise, use a largish pan
with a lid. Melt the butter in the pan. Break up
the vermicelli, and brown it in the butter, stirring
with a wooden spoon. Add the ground wheat
(bulgour) and stir while it rapidly absorbs the
butter. Pour in the hot stock or water, stir well
and, putting the lid on, turn the heat as low as
you can. Let it cook undisturbed for 12 minutes,
when all the liquid should be absorbed. Stir again,
and replace lid. Remove from heat and leave it
alone for another 12 minutes. Stir it again and leave
it for 5 minutes. Serve with seasoning of more
pepper than salt, sprinkled with parsley, and if
liked, a spoonful of yoghurt with each helping.

□ *Similar to couscous, it goes well with stews.*

For 6–8

To Cook Dried Beans or Lentils

white, green, red, brown or black, large or small
beans, 3 oz per person
water
bouquet of parsley, thyme, bayleaf, celery stalk and
  garlic if liked
salt

Soak the beans for several hours, at least four and
at most twelve or overnight; any longer and they will
start to ferment. Drain and put in a saucepan with
enough cold water to come two inches above the
top of the beans. Add *no salt* but put in the herbs
and garlic (and a piece of salt pork or bacon if you
like). Bring slowly to the boil and cook gently until
the beans are tender, a minimum of one hour and
up to two, depending on how long ago they were
picked and dried. If they take longer than this the
chances are they will never be tender.

Add salt about 15 minutes before draining the
beans. Keep the liquid for soup. They are now
ready for whatever you want to do with them. They
can be served as they are with plenty of freshly
chopped parsley and butter; or bathed in a sauce of
tomatoes and onion cooked in oil with a cupful of
their own liquid; or stirred into a creamy sauce
made with butter, flour and their own liquid, plus
chopped parsley; or you can leave out the
parsley but add chopped boiled bacon or ham.

Cold, they make very good salads with vinaigrette
dressing and raw onion, tuna fish, green beans or
just parsley.

Haricot and French Bean Salad

½ lb large white haricot beans (dried)
1 onion
2 cloves garlic
1 lb French beans
1 tablespoon white wine vinegar
5–6 tablespoons olive oil
½ Spanish onion
parsley, chopped
salt and freshly ground pepper

Dhal

½ lb small orange lentils
1 onion
1 clove of garlic } peeled and chopped
1 oz butter, or margarine and oil
1 teaspoon tomato purée
½ teaspoon coriander powder
½ teaspoon cumin seed
salt

Soak the beans for about 5–6 hours. Put them in a pan and cover well with cold water, put in the peeled onion and the cloves of garlic. Bring slowly to the boil, skim and simmer for about ¾ hour. Add salt and simmer on for a quarter of an hour or so. When tender but not mushy, drain and cool. Cook the French beans, broken in pieces if they are too long, in boiling salted water for 10–15 minutes. When just tender, strain and refresh quickly under the cold tap. Drain very well. Mix the two kinds of beans together. Make an oily dressing with plenty of freshly ground pepper, and mix it in carefully so as not to break up the haricots. Strew some rings of Spanish onion on top and some chopped parsley if you like.

☐ *This is a very pretty dish.*

For 6

Cover the lentils (they don't need soaking) with double their volume of water. They will cook quite quickly and absorb most of it. In another pan, fry the onion and garlic lightly in the butter until transparent. Add the tomato purée, spices and some salt. Stir. Add the lentils, which should not be too runny. Mix all well together and cook until the flavours are absorbed by the lentils (5–10 minutes). This will reheat well. If it is too stiff, add hot water.

☐ *For eating with curries.*

For 4

Leeks in Red Wine

10 leeks, the same size and not too large
2 tablespoons olive oil
1 glass red wine
½ pint boiling water or stock
salt

Trim the leeks and wash well. Drain and shake them as dry as possible. Heat the oil in a wide shallow pan with room for all the leeks side by side. Gently brown them all over, pour on the wine and let it bubble a minute or two. Add salt and boiling stock or water, cover the pan and cook until the leeks are tender (test by piercing the root end with a sharp knife).

Take out the leeks with a perforated spoon and put them on a hot serving dish. Reduce the liquid a little and pour it over. These are particularly good with roast meat or chicken.

For 4

Leeks Vinaigrette

1 ½ lbs of the smallest leeks you can buy
5 dessertspoons olive oil
1 ½ dessertspoons white wine vinegar
salt and freshly ground pepper
Dijon mustard
garlic

Clean and trim the leeks, keeping the firm white part and the best of the green.

Bring a pan of salted water to the boil, drop in the leeks and let them cook until just tender. Put in a colander and leave to drain and cool.

Mash a clove of garlic with salt, mix with a teaspoon of mustard and plenty of pepper. Add 1½ dessertspoons of vinegar and mix in thoroughly. Now add the oil, mixing gradually — it thickens like mayonnaise. You will need about 5 dessertspoons of oil but taste from time to time until it is right. When the leeks are thoroughly drained, lay them on a plate all in the same direction. Pour on the dressing and turn them a couple of times. They look very good on a white oval or oblong dish.

☐ *Serve these as an hors d'oeuvre or salad.*

For 2–4

Mushrooms à la Grecque

¾ lb fresh button mushrooms
4 tablespoons olive oil
4 tablespoons water
juice of ½ lemon
1 teaspoon coriander seeds
salt and freshly ground pepper
bayleaf, thyme, parsley

Raw Mushroom Salad

½ lb tiny button mushrooms
¼ pint sour cream
½ lemon
salt and freshly ground pepper

Boil together in a wide shallow pan the oil, water, lemon juice, coriander seeds, seasoning and a large bunch of herbs, for ten minutes. Clean the mushrooms, and if they are small add them whole to the liquid, if large, quarter them first. They must be closed and round; open ones absorb too much liquid, and exude too much so they end up sloppy.

Simmer the mushrooms slowly for ten minutes, stirring, then remove them to a dish and reduce the liquid a little. Pour it over the mushrooms, when the herbs and coriander seeds will be stranded on top. Leave them there, they look lovely and improve the flavour. Let the mushrooms get cold and eat with coarse brown bread and unsalted butter. They do shrink terribly but they don't need to be eaten in large quantities. Serve them with other salads as an hors d'oeuvre. They are good with cold cooked lentils in an oil and vinegar dressing, or with courgettes done in the same way as the mushrooms but with tomatoes instead of water added to the sauce.

For 4

Trim the mushrooms, and if they are the slightest bit bruised or brown, peel them. As you peel each one, rub it with a cut lemon. When they are all ready slice each one down into very thin slices. Keep the stalks on so that each slice shows a tiny mushroom in section.

Put them into a white china or earthenware bowl and mix in the sour cream; season lightly. This should be a very delicate salad. If you like you can add a little more lemon juice to sharpen it up.

☐ *This is one of the prettiest salads there is.*

For 3

Field Mushrooms

mushrooms
butter
top of the milk
salt
pepper

Mushrooms with Brown Rice

½ lb mushrooms
4 oz brown rice
1 oz butter
parsley
3 cloves garlic
salt and freshly ground pepper

Clean and slice the mushrooms, melt the butter in a frying pan and fry them gently. As they absorb the butter, add a saucerful of creamy milk. Continue cooking for about ten minutes; they will then take more milk. This, rather than being absorbed, will thicken a little, leaving the mushrooms in a delicate creamy sauce. Add salt and pepper to taste and eat at once with egg and bacon or toast.

☐ *The quantities depend on how many mushrooms you find.*

Soak the brown rice in salted water overnight, strain and rinse. Put it in fresh salted water and cook gently until tender, 15–20 minutes. The grains should still be separate and have a slight bite to them.

Meanwhile slice the mushrooms and put them in a sauté pan with the butter. Let them cook very, very slowly so that the juices all run out; stir from time to time. Chop the parsley and garlic finely. Stir the drained rice and the parsley and garlic into the mushrooms, season, let it get really hot and then serve with stewed lamb or beef or roast lamb.

For 4

Really Crisp Fried Onions

Spanish onions
salt
flour
deep fat or oil

Pommes de Terre Rissolées

2 lbs new potatoes the size of a walnut
2–3 oz butter, preferably clarified (page 220) or
    unsalted
coarse salt

Slice the onions into thin rings and separate each one. Sprinkle lightly with fine salt and let them stand for an hour or so, for the moisture to drain off. Toss them in flour and drop them into hot fat or oil (with blue haze rising). As soon as they are golden brown take them out and drain them on kitchen paper. Eat as they are or with hamburgers etc.

Scrape the potatoes, and dry each one thoroughly on a cloth. Melt the butter in a large heavy saucepan and fry the potatoes, turning them over and over so they brown evenly. When they are nicely golden turn the heat right down and cover the saucepan. Let them cook gently like this for an hour. When the potatoes are tender, and easily pierced with a skewer, turn up the heat and shake the pan until they are crisp on the outside. It may take several minutes, so take care not to burn the butter at this point. As soon as they are crisp, sprinkle with plenty of coarse salt, and serve. They don't always end up absolutely crisp, but they do always end up absolutely delicious.

□ *This is a recipe for small new potatoes; very good with any plainly roasted or braised poultry or meat.*

For 6

Potato Crisps

1 large potato
salt
deep oil for frying

Perfect Mashed Potatoes

1½ lbs good floury potatoes such as King Edwards,
  not Majestic
½ pint milk
2 oz butter
salt, freshly ground pepper, and a grating of nutmeg

Peel and slice the potato as thinly as possible. This is quickly done on a cucumber slicer or mandoline.

Wash the potato slices under the cold tap as you cut them, to remove the loose starch granules, and keep them all in cold water until you have finished the slicing. Then dry well in a cloth, shaking them as if you were drying a salad. Keep them in the cloth until ready to start frying.

Heat the oil in a pan with a deep-frying basket; when a blue haze rises test one slice. If it comes straight up to the surface, sizzling, the oil is ready. Lift the basket out of the oil, holding it over the pan fill it with two handfuls of crisps, and lower it back into the oil. If you put in too many crisps there is a great danger of the oil boiling over, so be very careful at this point and whisk the basket out if the oil starts to rise too far. As soon as the crisps *start* to colour lift the basket out of the oil while you count ten, then put it back again. As they turn golden lift them out, let them drain, and put them in a dish lined with kitchen paper to dry, sprinkling with fine salt.

They keep crisp in polythene bags.

Cook the potatoes in boiling salted water. It doesn't matter whether you peel the potatoes before or after they are cooked, but they should be more or less the same size and cooked very thoroughly indeed. Once they are peeled, cooked and drained, put them back in the saucepan over a very low heat to dry out for a minute. Mash with a fork or potato masher, or for real perfection put them through the mouli, before adding *hot* milk and butter, beating with a fork or wooden spoon as you go. Season with salt, pepper and nutmeg. The result should be really light. If it seems too dry add more milk and butter.

For 4

German Potato Dropscones

¼ lb potatoes, peeled
¼ lb plain flour and 1 heaped teaspoon baking
   powder, or ¼ lb self-raising flour
2 eggs, separated
1 tablespoon oil or melted butter
¼ pint or less of milk
salt

Grate the raw potatoes. Squeeze out some of their liquid and put them into a bowl. Mix at once with the flour and baking powder. Incorporate the egg yolks, butter or oil, milk and a little salt. Whip the egg whites stiffly, and fold into the mixture. Heat and grease the griddle (see dropscones, page 213).

Drop spoonfuls of the mixture on to the griddle, giving them about three minutes on each side. Serve with eggs and bacon. They are also good spread with butter.

☐ *Eat these for breakfast or tea.*

About 20 scones

Potato Cakes

mashed potato
1 beaten egg
self-raising flour, not more than half as much as
   potato
salt and freshly ground pepper
bacon fat or beef dripping

Mix the potatoes, egg, flour and seasoning to make a firm dough. Roll out to about half an inch thick and cut into rounds. Fry well, in hot fat quarter of an inch deep in the frying pan. Delicious for breakfast, with egg and bacon, or for children's high tea. Surprisingly, creamy mashed potato is less successful than dry mashed potato.

☐ *The number depends on the amount of left-over mashed potato you have.*

Champ

2 lbs potatoes
¼—½ pint milk
butter
salt and pepper
10 spring onions
bunch parsley

Peel and cut up the potatoes, and cook them with plenty of salt for a bit too long, until they are really soft but not disintegrating. It takes about 25 minutes. Meanwhile chop the spring onions and parsley as finely as you can, and heat the milk. When the potatoes are done, drain them and mash them with the boiling milk, pepper and more salt if necessary, plus butter if you like. When they are finely puréed add the chopped onions and parsley and mash these in. The potatoes should still be moist enough to fall off the spoon when you give it a shake.

This is an Irish potato dish which you could practically eat on its own. It is also very good with fish or any plain roasted meat.

For 6

Persian Rice

3 oz rice per person
2 oz butter
1 tablespoon salt

Pour a kettle of boiling water over the rice in a sieve. Separate the grains and soak for three or four hours in cold water. Wash thoroughly and put in a large pan with copious amounts of cold water and a tablespoon of salt. Boil for exactly eight minutes, until the rice is almost, but not quite, tender. Wash again under the cold tap and drain.

Put one ounce of melted butter in a flameproof casserole and put in the drained rice. Pour over another ounce of melted butter, cover with a cloth and then with the casserole lid. Put over a very low flame for 15–20 minutes. Each grain is separate, perfectly cooked and delicious. At the bottom of the pan is a golden crust which is much sought after by the Persians.

This is a complicated way of rice-cooking, but very good. You can leave out some of the soaking, if you don't have time.

□ *Use Basmati or best Patna rice. These are the best quality, long-grain rices and more likely to cook to perfection than nameless packets or semi-prepared brands.*

For 4–6

Risotto Milanese

12 oz Italian rice
2–3 tablespoons olive oil
1 small onion, chopped
small glass white wine
pinch saffron
¾–1 pint bouillon or light stock, heated
salt and freshly ground pepper
knob of butter
2–3 oz Parmesan, freshly grated

Heat the oil in a fairly large sauté pan with a lid, and fry the onion gently until it is transparent. Add the rice and stir with a wooden spoon, until it too is transparent. Stir the saffron into the wine and add it to the rice; let it sizzle, then add ¾ pint of hot stock, turn the heat low, cover and leave it to cook about 15 minutes. Check that it is not sticking to the bottom; if it is, it needs another cup of stock or water.

After 20–30 minutes the rice should be quite soft, and all the liquid absorbed. Stir in the lump of butter and a spoonful or two of grated Parmesan. Serve with more butter and Parmesan on each helping, and some black pepper. It is very good on its own, but you can serve it with kebabs or chicken livers (page 49).

For 4

Raïta

½ large cucumber or 1 small whole one
1 clove garlic
small sprig mint
½ teaspoon salt
1 5-oz pot plain yoghurt

Peel the cucumber, then, according to how you like it, grate it or cut it in small cubes or sticks; thin round slices don't suit this dish at all.

Crush the garlic in a garlic crusher or chop as finely as you can. Slice the mint leaves finely. Sprinkle the cucumber with the mint, garlic and salt and leave it to drain in a strainer for half an hour.

Put it in a bowl, mix with the yoghurt and chill until needed. In India it is usually grated; in Greece cut in little chunks. You can skip the half hour's draining if in a hurry, but don't wait too long before eating it or the yoghurt will become watery. The draining also makes it more digestible.

☐ *A soothing dish to accompany curry and also a cool summer salad.*

For 2

Salade au Lard

Chicory, young spinach leaves, dandelion, endive,
   or watercress
Vinaigrette dressing (page 186)
1 rasher of bacon per person

Wash the salad leaves and dry well. Trim the rind
off the bacon and cut into little sticks about half an
inch long. Fry the rinds slowly in a frying pan to
extract the fat; when it starts to run remove the
rinds and fry the bacon pieces until crisp and brown,
while you are making a slightly vinegary dressing;
don't add much salt, the bacon will do this.

Toss the salad in the dressing and at the last moment
pour the bacon and its fat over everything. Mix
well and serve with the bacon still hot.

For any number

Spinach and Chick Peas

½ lb chick peas
salt
1 lb spinach
1 tablespoon paprika
2 tablespoons olive oil
1 slice bread
1 onion, chopped
3–4 tomatoes, peeled and chopped
1 clove garlic

Soak the chick peas overnight and cook as on page
156. When they are tender, fry the slice of bread
golden in oil. Put the fried bread on one side while
you fry the onions, then the tomatoes. Wash
the spinach, shake it and sprinkle it with salt.
Heat two tablespoons of oil in a large pan, add the
paprika and stir it in. Add the spinach and when
it is lightly fried, put the mixture into a saucepan
with the chick peas, onions and tomatoes.

Pound the clove of garlic, add the fried bread and
pound it thoroughly. Add this mixture to the chick
peas. Cover and simmer for half an hour, when you
will have a fragrant vegetable stew, thickened and
interestingly flavoured by the pounded fried bread.

☐ *Very good for a cold day.*

For 3–4

Spinach with Tomato Sauce

1 lb spinach
½ lb tomatoes
salt and freshly ground pepper
pinch sugar
1 small onion, chopped
1–2 oz butter
butter and oil for frying

Wash the spinach very well, shake off most of the water and cook in a covered pan with the moisture still clinging to the leaves, until tender, 10–15 minutes. Drain off the water it has made, chop and stir in the butter and a little salt.

While the spinach is cooking, skin and chop the tomatoes. Sweat the chopped onion in a little butter and oil, without browning, for 10–15 minutes. Add the tomatoes, salt, pepper and sugar to taste. Let it simmer into a rough purée, stirring from time to time.

Serve the spinach with a little dollop of tomato sauce in the centre of each helping, so it looks like a red and green fried egg.

It is a suprisingly good combination of tastes.

For 2

Spinach Tart

2 lbs fresh spinach
1 oz butter
1 oz flour
½ pint creamy milk
2 cloves garlic
1 oz grated Parmesan
butter
salt and freshly ground pepper
9 oz flan pastry (page 218)

Make the pastry well in advance and keep it in a cool place. Cook the washed spinach in the water still clinging to the leaves, with a good sprinkling of salt. Make a smooth Béchamel sauce with the butter flour and milk; season it and add the crushed cloves of garlic and most of the cheese. Drain the spinach when it is well cooked, squeezing out the water very thoroughly, and chop slightly. Meanwhile butter a 7–8 inch flan case and line it with pastry. Bake this shell blind (page 217).

Mix the spinach into the sauce, pour into the flan case and sprinkle with the remaining cheese. Bake at Reg 4/350° for 15–20 minutes and brown the top briefly under the grill, dotting it with butter first.

☐ *This is a very good hot lunch dish; eaten cold it is marvellous for a picnic.*

For 4

Mashed Swede

1 large swede
salt and pepper
sugar
1 oz butter
orange juice

Baked Swede

1 swede, peeled and cubed
2 oz butter
½ teaspoon salt
½ teaspoon sugar

Peel the swede, removing all the fibrous pieces. Cut into one-inch cubes, cover with cold water, add salt and cook 20–25 minutes. Drain the swede, mash carefully, add pepper, a little more salt if necessary, a sprinkling of sugar, the butter and, if you like, a squeeze of orange juice. Heat through and serve. Children seem to like this as much as carrots.

For 4–6

Butter a small casserole with a close-fitting lid. Sprinkle the salt on to the cubed swede, and put it into the casserole, dotted with the remaining butter. Sprinkle with the sugar, cover very tightly with foil and the lid, for you add no water, and bake in a low oven, or the bottom of a warm oven, for 1½ hours.

☐ *People with an aversion to mashed swede seem to gobble this up.*

For 4

To Peel and De-seed Tomatoes

Stuffed Tomatoes

6 large or 12 small tomatoes
2 oz butter
2 oz fresh breadcrumbs
12 leaves of basil or 1 teaspoon dried basil
6 black olives, stoned and chopped
2–3 cloves garlic
salt and freshly ground pepper

Put the kettle on. Put the tomatoes (without their stalks) in a deep bowl. When the kettle boils, pour the water over them. Scoop them out one at a time with a spoon and peel them as quickly as you can. If there are a great many to skin, do them in several batches, as standing in hot water makes them mushy.

If you only have one or two tomatoes to peel, and a gas cooker, stick them on a fork and hold them over a burner. Turn the flame up high and turn the tomato in it until the skin pops, singes and splits; it will then peel off quite easily.

To remove the seeds: cut the tomato in half and hold one half in the palm of your hand. Squeezing it slightly, give it a brisk shake and the seeds will flop out.

To draw out the excess moisture: if you want to make stuffed tomatoes you can get rid of some of the water by sprinkling the insides of the halves with salt and leaving them upside-down to drain for half an hour or so.

Melt the butter and mix it into the breadcrumbs. Add the finely chopped olives and basil, crushed cloves of garlic, salt and pepper. Mix together well.

Cut the tomatoes in half across their equators. Empty out the seeds (see this page) and put a generous teaspoon of stuffing in each, pressing it down with the back of the spoon. Bake at Reg 3/325° for one hour in an earthenware dish or baking tin. There is no need to oil or butter the dish in which they are cooked. Serve them hot or cold.

☐ *These are to eat with lamb etc. or even on their own.*

For 6

Tomato and Mozzarella Salad

4 tomatoes
1 Mozzarella cheese
basil or oregano
salt and freshly ground pepper
oil and vinegar

Slice the cheese into rounds and lay a slice of tomato on top of each, or lay in overlapping lines, alternating tomato and Mozzarella, on a dish. Sprinkle with fresh or dried basil or oregano. Serve straight away with oil, vinegar, salt and pepper.

☐ *This is a very Italian salad. Eat it as a first course.*

For 2

Plain Tomato Salad

1 lb firm, under- rather than over-ripe tomatoes
1 small onion
salt and pepper
2–3 tablespoons olive oil
sprinkling of fresh chopped parsley, basil or chives

You need not bother to peel them, but if you want a very delicate salad dip the tomatoes in boiling water as briefly as possible and skin them quickly. Slice them thinly across and lay the slices on a plate. Sprinkle lightly with salt. Treat the onions, also thinly sliced, in the same way.

When they have stood in the salt for $\frac{1}{2}$–1 hour, tip the plates and drain off the juices. Rinse the onions, dry them, and scatter them over the tomatoes. Sprinkle with parsley and chives or basil. Add the oil and a turn of pepper, and serve chilled. Don't let it stand too long or the tomatoes lose their firm texture.

For 4

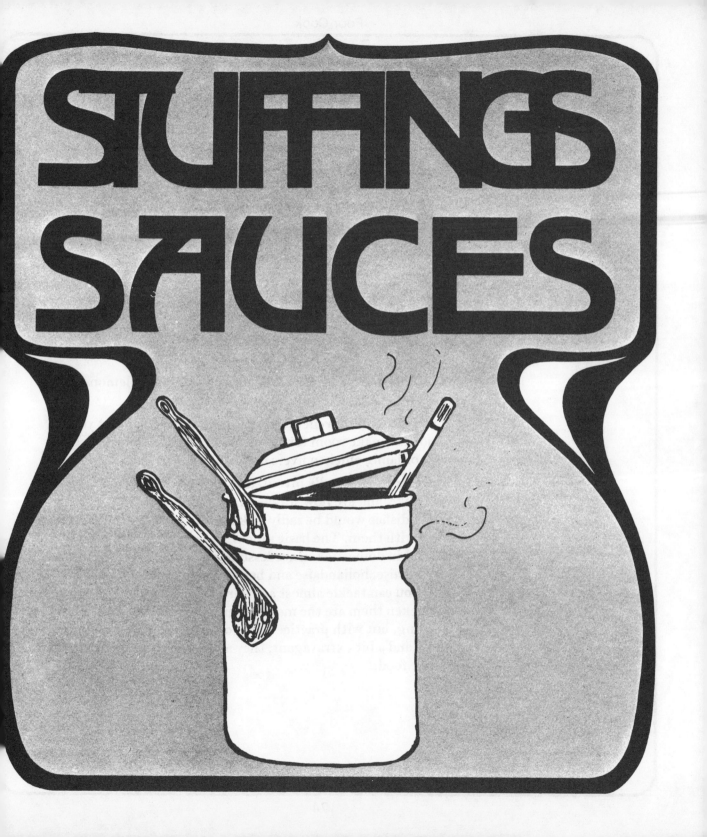

STUFFINGS
SAUCES

Stuffings and Sauces

It is a bore making a stuffing when you are roasting a bird, but it is worth it when you find it later, a bonus as it were. Not only turkeys deserve this treatment; some fish and lots of vegetables take well to a stuffing, and so of course do chickens and boned shoulders and breasts of lamb and veal. Even a cut onion or lemon and a bunch of herbs help to keep a bird moist, but if you are going in for the real bona fide filling-stuffing you can choose from these categories, using a combination that suits the dish:

(1) To keep it moist: bacon, mushrooms, onions, celery, apples, prunes.

(2) To pad it out: breadcrumbs, rice, oats, cracked wheat, sausage meat.

(3) To bind it: stock, tomato purée, butter, olive oil, egg, wine, milk, suet.

(4) To flavour it: garlic, herbs, seasoning, spices, lemon peel or juice, pine nuts, chestnuts, almonds, raisins.

If you are stuffing vegetables, use part of the flesh that you remove to make room for the stuffing, and add minced beef, pork or lamb, chicken livers or diced bacon or ham.

Sauces were originally invented to disguise what the food was really like, and are now supposed to complement it. Certainly lots of dishes would be sadly lacking love if no sauce was made to go with them. The basic sauces are the very first things to be learned in domestic science lessons, and once you have béchamel, mayonnaise, hollandaise and basic tomato sauce under your belt, you can tackle almost anything. Sauces which use egg yolks to thicken them are the most difficult to handle because of the curdling, but with practice they go quite fast, and although fiddly and a bit extravagant, they add a great touch of luxury to simple food.

Marjoram Stuffing for Chicken

½ onion, finely chopped
2 thick slices white bread
1½ teaspoons chopped fresh marjoram, or 1 teaspoon
    dried
2 tablespoons softened butter
salt

Soften the onion in a little butter until transparent
but not brown. Cut the crusts off the bread and
grate to make fairly coarse crumbs. Mix these with
the onion and its butter, and the marjoram, salt and
softened butter. Stuff the bird with this mixture
and roast in the usual way.

Don't press the stuffing in too firmly as it should be
very light.

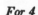 *In France this stuffing is often used with guinea-fowl.*

For 4

Stuffing for a Roast Chicken

The chicken's liver (only if pink or reddish), chopped
1 medium onion, chopped
2 oz bulgour (ground wheat), boiled in salted water
    5 minutes
1 oz softened butter
½ teaspoon grated lemon rind
salt and freshly ground pepper

Fry all the ingredients together for a few minutes;
stuff the mixture into the bird.

Spinach Stuffing

1 lb spinach
1 clove garlic
¼ lb minced pork
salt and freshly ground pepper
1 small egg (optional)
½ oz butter

Cook the spinach and squeeze it dry. Purée it and
let it sit in a sieve while you sauté the minced pork
in the butter in a saucepan for a few minutes.
Pulverise the garlic clove and add it and the spinach
to the pork in the saucepan. Take it off the heat and
add salt, pepper and the beaten egg, or half of it
if the mixture appears to be getting too sloppy. It is
rather a wet stuffing anyway, but becomes firm in
the cooking.

☐ *Excellent for boned shoulder or breast of lamb*
(*page 116*).

Aïoli

3–4 cloves garlic
2 egg yolks
¼ pint olive oil
salt and pepper
a few drops of vinegar or lemon juice

Make this exactly like mayonnaise but thoroughly
pulverise the garlic cloves with salt and stir them
into the egg yolks before you start to add the oil.
Don't use much lemon or vinegar in the making of
aïoli as it should be very thick.

☐ *For raw vegetables, fish soup, boiled vegetables,*
boiled chicken and cold chicken.

Apple Sauce

2–4 apples, peeled, quartered and cored
1 tablespoon water
1 tablespoon white sugar
2 cloves
squeeze lemon juice
½ oz butter

Put all the ingredients in a pan and cook until the apple is tender. Remove the cloves. Beat to a smooth purée and serve hot.

☐ *For pork.*

Bread Sauce

½ pint milk
1 onion, peeled
5 cloves
2 blades of mace
2–3 slices of white bread, at least an inch thick
salt, pepper and a grating of nutmeg
walnut-sized knob of butter

Stick the cloves into the onion and put it in a small saucepan with the milk and blades of mace. Stand this on an asbestos mat over a very low heat, and let it infuse for up to one hour without boiling. Remove the onion and mace. Cut the crusts off the bread and crumble it into the milk, whisking with a fork. Season with salt, pepper and nutmeg, and if you like add the finely chopped onion with the cloves removed. Heat it without boiling and, just before serving, stir in the butter.

☐ *For roasted birds.*

Béchamel Sauce

1 oz butter
1 oz flour
½ pint milk
salt, pepper

Egg Sauce

¼ pint well-flavoured thin Béchamel, made with
    half milk and half fish- or chicken-stock
2 hard-boiled eggs
salt and white pepper

Heat the milk to just below boiling point (see note below on infusion). Melt the butter in a small saucepan over a moderate heat without browning. Tip in the flour and stir to amalgamate it with the butter. This mixture is called a white roux and should not be allowed to brown. When it starts to honeycomb, i.e. when small bubbles start to break all over the surface of the mixture, pour in one third of the milk, stirring vigorously until you have a smooth mixture. When it has thickened into a smooth paste add one third more milk. Stir again and when it has thickened gradually add the rest of the milk until you have a smooth sauce of the consistency you require. Season and cook very gently, stirring from time to time, for five minutes, to cook the flour. The best Béchamel is made with milk which you have previously infused with various flavourings to make it tastier. Simply put a small sliced onion, a bayleaf, a small bunch of parsley and a few peppercorns into the cold milk, bring it to boiling point, turn the heat right down and let the milk stand just not boiling over a very low flame for up to half an hour. Strain the milk before you make the sauce.

☐ *This makes ½ pint, medium thick sauce.*

Sieve the egg yolks into the Béchamel, chop the whites and add these too. The Béchamel should be of a creamy consistency so that the egg whites are visible as a texture in the sauce. Season and serve hot. This has become almost a joke because it smacks of institutions, but made properly it is a good English sauce of quality.

☐ *A delicate sauce for chicken, fishcakes and steamed cod, turbot or halibut.*

Sauce Hollandaise

2 tablespoons white wine vinegar
1 tablespoon water
2–3 peppercorns
½ bayleaf
1 blade mace
1 large egg yolk
4–5 oz slightly salted butter

Cut the butter into small cubes and if it is very
hard let it soften a bit. Put the vinegar, water,
peppercorns, bayleaf and mace into a small
saucepan and reduce to half their quantity. Allow
to cool and remove peppercorns, bayleaf and mace.
Take a double saucepan, or a pan into which a
suitable bowl or basin will fit, and heat some water
in it to just below boiling point. In order to lessen
the risk of the sauce curdling keep the water below
the boil, and make sure it doesn't actually touch
the base of the bowl or pan in which the sauce is
cooking. Using the bowl or pan which is to go over
the water, mix the reduced vinegar and water with
the egg yolk and a cube of the soft butter. Place
it over the hot water and stirring all the time with
a wooden spoon, add the cubes of butter one at a
time, letting each one melt before you add another.
If the sauce shows signs of thickening too fast, or
curdling, remove it at once from the water. If it
is too thick add a few drops of water or the top of
the milk. Taste for salt. If it is too sharp add some
unsalted butter. It should be smooth and fairly
thick, and is served lukewarm.

☐ *For serving with Oeufs Bénédictine and poached
fish (and asparagus).*

Horseradish Sauce

1–2 tablespoons grated horseradish
½ teaspoon salt
½ teaspoon mustard powder
1 teaspoon white sugar
1 dessertspoon wine vinegar or lemon juice
2–3 tablespoons thin cream or top of the milk

Mix all well together. The grating of fresh horseradish is far more of a torture than cutting up
onions, but the result is really worth it. Beware if you
start growing it in the garden; it must be confined,
otherwise the whole garden will soon be covered
with what is virtually an indestructible weed.

☐ *For hot or cold roast beef, or herrings.*

Mayonnaise

1 egg yolk
scant ¼ pint olive oil
salt and white pepper
1 teaspoon lemon juice or white wine vinegar

Green Mayonnaise

¼ pint very thick mayonnaise (this page)
handful of young spinach leaves
handful of watercress
4–5 sprigs parsley
fresh tarragon if available

Put the egg yolk, *not* straight out of the refrigerator, with the seasoning, into a bowl and beat it with a wooden fork or spoon. Put the oil into a jug with a narrow lip, or an oil bottle with a spout, so that you can drip it out in minute drops. Start adding the oil to the egg yolk a few drops at a time, beating continuously. When the mixture starts to thicken, add a few drops of vinegar or lemon juice, then continue trickling in the oil, adding a little more at a time as it gets thicker, until you are pouring it in a thin thread-like stream, and stirring all the time. Add more vinegar or lemon as necessary. If the egg yolk is small it may not take quarter of a pint of oil; when threads of oil appear in the lines left by the fork or spoon, be very cautious about adding more or it may curdle. When it is finished it can be thinned with cream, top of the milk or warm water to make a pouring consistency for egg mayonnaise etc. If you do curdle your mayonnaise, break a fresh egg yolk into a separate bowl, beat it, and add the curdled lot, *a little at a time,* until it is all worked in.

For 2–3

Blanch all the greenery for two or three minutes in boiling salted water. Squeeze dry and pulverize. You should now have a dark green purée. Put it in a fine sieve to drain the water off.

Just before serving stir it carefully into the mayonnaise. It makes the most beautiful speckled, pale green sauce.

☐ *Use instead of plain mayonnaise; it is more special because it looks so marvellous, especially with cold fish and hard-boiled eggs.*

Mustard Sauce

¼ pint Hollandaise sauce (page 179)
1–2 teaspoons made English mustard

Make the Hollandaise and when finished stir in one
or two teaspoons freshly made mustard.

For 2

Mustard Sauce 2

¼ pint double cream
1 teaspoon made mustard
salt and freshly ground pepper

Mix the ingredients together and pour over
open filleted cooked fish.

☐ *These sauces are marvellous with fried or grilled
herring, mackerel or sprats, and with tongue.*

For 4

Mint Sauce

¼ pint wine vinegar
1½ oz Demerara sugar
1 tablespoon finely chopped mint

Bring the vinegar to the boil in a small pan, and
dissolve the Demerara sugar in it. Put the mint in a
bowl and pour on the boiling vinegar. Allow it to
cool.

☐ *For lamb*

Pizzaiola Sauce

1 lb tomatoes, fresh or tinned, skinned and chopped
2 tablespoons oil
1 clove garlic, sliced
salt, pepper and a pinch of sugar
handful of parsley, chopped
½ handful of fresh basil or oregano, chopped

Heat the oil in a small frying pan and brown the garlic. Add the tomatoes, salt, pepper and sugar and cook, stirring, for 10–15 minutes. Add the freshly chopped herbs and serve.

☐ *For fish, pasta, steaks, chops, kebabs.*

Sauce Soubise (onion sauce)

½ lb onions
2 tablespoons butter
2 tablespoons flour
½ pint creamy milk or light, good stock
salt, pepper and nutmeg
pinch of sugar

Peel and slice the onions finely and stew them gently in the butter in a saucepan for 10–15 minutes. They must not brown. Stir in the flour, cook for one minute, then gradually add the heated milk or stock, stirring as it thickens. Season and simmer for 15–20 minutes taking care not to let the sauce catch at the bottom. Sieve or liquidise the mixture, taste for seasoning and sugar and serve hot.

☐ *For roast lamb and lamb chops, and for Oeufs à la Tripe (page 42).*

Rouille

2 red pimentos, bottled or tinned will do
4 cloves garlic, peeled
1 slice white bread, crusts removed
salt to taste
2 tablespoons olive oil
2 tablespoons broth from the fish soup (page 72)

Cut up the peppers, remove the seeds and pound them with the garlic and crumbled bread and a little salt. Gradually add the oil and broth until you have a smooth sauce. It is hot because of the quantity of garlic, so if your cloves are very small use more.

☐ *For fish soup or boiled fish.*

Red Sauce

2 tablespoons fresh white breadcrumbs
2 tablespoons wine vinegar
2 cloves garlic
2 large ripe tomatoes, skinned and de-seeded
  (page 171)
large pinch salt and paprika
6 tablespoons olive oil

Soak the breadcrumbs in the vinegar. Pound the garlic in a mortar and add the tomatoes and breadcrumbs. Season with salt and paprika and add the olive oil gradually, until the sauce is thick.

☐ *This is a Spanish sauce whose ingredients sound unlikely, but it is delicious, especially with cold fish or shellfish, hard-boiled eggs, or with a plain potato salad instead of dressing or mayonnaise.*

For 4

Sauce Béarnaise

4 tablespoons wine vinegar
1 shallot
1 bayleaf
1 blade of mace
6 peppercorns
2 large egg yolks
4 oz fresh butter
1 heaped teaspoon of chopped tarragon, chervil and
     parsley, mixed
salt and freshly ground pepper

Reduce the vinegar with the spices to a tablespoon.
Work the yolks with a nut of the softened butter,
strain the vinegar over them, stir and thicken in a
bain-marie, gradually adding the rest of the butter
stirring constantly. Add the herbs and seasoning.

☐ *For grilled fish or meat.*

Cumberland Sauce

4 oranges
2 lemons
2 small shallots
1 dessertspoon fresh English or Dijon mustard
3 tablespoons cheap wine or wine vinegar
1 large glass cheap port
1 lb redcurrant jelly
salt and freshly ground pepper

Peel the oranges and lemons very thinly with a
potato peeler, so that the pieces of peel have no
pith. Cut the peel into tiny thin strips, cover them
with cold water in a small pan, bring to the boil and
then strain immediately. Peel and chop the shallots
very finely, put in a small pan, cover with cold water,
boil for a few minutes and strain. Mix the mustard,
wine, port and the juice of the lemons and of two of
the oranges. (Use more orange juice if they aren't
very juicy). Stir in the redcurrant jelly and dissolve
it slowly over a low heat. Add the peel and shallots
and a generous seasoning of salt and pepper. Simmer
20 minutes or more until it thickens a bit, pour into
small jars and keep in the fridge. It keeps a week or
two and makes a good Christmas present. It has a
very sweet spicy flavour.

☐ *For cold ham, duck, turkey or game.*

Chilli Tomato Sauce

1 onion, finely chopped
2 red chilli peppers or 1 teaspoon chilli powder
   (more if liked)
1 lb tomatoes, skinned and chopped
3–4 cloves garlic, peeled and chopped finely
salt and freshly ground pepper
thyme, sage and parsley tied in a bunch
butter and oil

Heat a little butter and oil in a frying pan, add the
onions and soften them. Stir in the chillies or chilli
powder, fry for a minute or two and then add the
tomatoes, garlic, seasoning and herbs.
Simmer uncovered until you have a thickish sauce,
remove the herbs and sieve or liquidise.

Reheat in the same pan before serving. This can be
ferociously or gently hot according to how much
chilli you put in.

☐ *A hot sauce, excellent with fried chicken.*

Tomato Sauce

2 onions
2 cloves garlic
2 tablespoons olive oil
1 ½ lbs tomatoes
½ glass red wine
sprigs of thyme and rosemary and a bayleaf
salt and freshly ground pepper

Chop the onions and garlic finely and soften them
in the oil in a saucepan for about ten minutes
without browning. Add the skinned roughly chopped
tomatoes, seasoning, red wine and bundle of herbs.
Simmer 45 minutes, uncovered.

☐ *For pasta, fried fish etc.*

For 6

Vinaigrette

4–5 tablespoons oil
½ teaspoon sea salt
several pinches freshly ground black pepper
1 teaspoon white sugar (optional)
2 teaspoons wine vinegar

Take a small bowl, mix the salt, pepper and sugar and add the oil. Then stir in the vinegar with a teaspoon; it should become thick and cloudy. Pour it over your green salad just as your serve it, and turn the leaves over until they glisten with oil. If you like garlic add a clove, first thoroughly pulverised with the salt, using the point of a stainless kitchen knife. If you only quite like it, put a few cubes of dried bread or rusk, thoroughly rubbed with cut cloves of garlic, into the bottom of the salad bowl. If you like a thick mustardy dressing, mix the vinegar with half a teaspoon of Dijon mustard and season this, leaving out the sugar, before you gradually add the oil.

☐ *For salads and cold vegetables.*

Vinaigrette à l'oeuf

vinaigrette (above)
1 small onion or shallot, chopped finely
a few chives, chopped
1 soft-boiled egg

Add the onion, chives and the yolk of the soft-boiled egg to the vinaigrette. Chop the white and add this too.

☐ *Good with boiled fowl or fish.*

Herb Butters

For serving with vegetables or grilled fish or meat. These herbs all make good fresh herb butters:
Mint: ideal for lamb, peas, new potatoes.
Parsley: for steak, fish or broad beans.
Tarragon: for potatoes, chicken or eggs.
Chives and parsley together: for steak, fish, lamb chops.
Rosemary: for lamb, pork, chicken, haricot beans.
Savory or Thyme: for grilled kidneys etc.

If you have a special chopping-bowl or a Mouli-Parsmint, chop the herbs in it, otherwise chop as finely as possible with a knife. Don't use more than one or two herbs, fresh and in generous amounts. For each person chop about one heaped teaspoon of herbs and mash it with a walnut of butter, a squeeze of lemon, salt and fresh ground pepper. Form into a one-inch roll in a piece of greaseproof paper, and put into the refrigerator to become firm. Place a half-inch slice of the roll on the food as you serve it.

Herb butters keep for up to a week in the refrigerator.

☐ *For serving with vegetables or grilled fish or meat.*

Puddings

This chapter concentrates mainly on puddings that children like, since many people now seem to want to go straight on to fresh fruit and cheese; but if your first course is nothing much, then a good pudding does help to salvage your reputation. One or two steamed puddings are included, and although they are a bit of a challenge to the modern stomach, they are comforting on a cold winter's day after a morning in the fresh air. Vanilla sugar is mentioned in several recipes; this is made by putting a vanilla pod into an airtight glass storage jar, and filling it up with caster sugar. Let it stay there, refilling with sugar when necessary, until it loses its aroma, which is only after several months. The flavour given by vanilla sugar is different and much better than the flavour of vanilla essence.

Rich Sweet Flan Pastry

6 oz plain flour
2 oz slightly salted butter
2 oz cooking fat
1 oz granulated sugar
1 egg yolk
a few drops cold water
pinch of salt

To Make and Bake a Fruit Flan

Sieve the flour and salt into a mixing bowl. Chop the butter and fat into small pieces in the flour. Add the sugar and rub it all together very lightly with your finger tips until it is integrated. Blend in the egg yolk, using a knife, and then add just a few drops of water to make it the consistency of soft, light marzipan. Leave it in a cool place wrapped in greaseproof paper, cloth, or polythene for at least three-quarters of an hour.

Preheat the oven to Reg 5$\frac{1}{2}$/390°. Press the pastry into an eight-inch loose flan ring, previously buttered, on a baking sheet, also buttered. It is too crumbly and sticky to roll out. Arrange the fruit (sliced apples or halved stoned apricots or plums) prettily in the flan. Sprinkle with sugar and bake ten minutes. Then lower heat and bake another 20 minutes at Reg 4$\frac{1}{2}$/360°. Allow to shrink and cool before sliding away the ring and lifting the tart with excruciating care on to a plate or dish. Glaze the top with syrup from in between the fruit, or with melted apricot jam.

☐ *See also page 217.*

Baked Apple Dumplings

½ lb flour
2 oz butter
2 oz cooking fat ⎫ for the pastry
pinch of salt
water to mix ⎭
4 medium-sized apples, peeled and cored
½ oz butter
1 oz Demerara sugar
1 teaspoon grated lemon rind (optional)

Make the pastry and let it stand in a cool place for at least half an hour. Preheat the oven to Reg 5/375° Peel and core the apples; mash the butter, sugar, and lemon rind, and stuff the apples with the mixture. Divide the pastry into four and roll out into four thin circles on a floured board. Place an apple on the centre of each (1); damp the edges and neatly bring the pastry up round each apple, pinching it together and trimming off any excess (2). Place the apples, joined side down, on a greased baking sheet, decorate the tops with pastry leaves and stalks (3), brush with water and sprinkle generously with caster sugar.

Bake the apples for 30 minutes and serve hot with cream.

For 4

Apple Crumble (or Apricot, or Blackberry and Apple)

1½ lbs cooking apples or apricots
or 1½ lbs blackberries and apples
sugar to sweeten the fruit
2 oz soft brown sugar
2 oz butter
4 oz plain flour
pinch of cinnamon

Preheat the oven to Reg 3/325°. Put the prepared fruit into a casserole with enough sugar to sweeten, cover and stew gently in the oven until the juice begins to run, or the apples begin to soften — 20–30 minutes.

Meanwhile rub the flour, butter, sugar and cinnamon together until the mixture looks like breadcrumbs. Take the fruit out of the oven, turn the oven up to Reg 6/400° and sprinkle the crumble mixture over the fruit. Return to the oven, uncovered, for 20 minutes, or until crisp and golden on top.

Serve hot with cream.

For 4

1

2

3

Apple Flan

2 lbs dessert apples (Golden Delicious are best)
½ small teaspoon powdered cinnamon
2 tablespoons brown sugar
2 tablespoons red wine vinegar
1 lb shortcrust pastry (page 189)

Preheat oven to Reg 5½/390°. Peel and slice the apples, and put them in a pan with the cinnamon, sugar and vinegar. Simmer covered, stirring occasionally, for half an hour; allow to cool. Line a seven-inch flan tin with a moveable base with two-thirds of the pastry. Fill with the apple mixture and cover with two-thirds of the remaining pastry. Decorate the top with a huge flower and bake in a moderate oven, Reg 5½/390°, for 30 minutes. Cover the top with sifted sugar when the pie has slightly cooled. The apples will be a wonderful golden brown and very spicy, and the vinegar flavour so delicate you could hardly tell.

For 5

Apple Fritters

4 apples
fritter batter (page 60)
ground cinnamon and cloves
caster sugar

Peel and core the apples and cut in rings. Press them with the sugar, mixed with the cinnamon and cloves, and then dip them into the batter. Deep-fry in hot oil and drain on kitchen paper. Sprinkle with caster sugar.

They are best served at once but can be kept warm in a low oven.

☐ *Cook banana or pineapple slices the same way.*

For 4–5

Fried Bananas

6 bananas, peeled and halved lengthwise
1½ oz butter
juice of half a lemon
Demerara sugar
1 tablespoon brandy, rum or liqueur
top of the milk or thin cream

Melt the butter in a large frying pan; as it foams put in the bananas. Brown them gently on each side for a few minutes, add the lemon juice and let it sizzle. Warm a spoonful of brandy or whatever, set light to it and pour, flaming, over the bananas. Sprinkle with Demerara sugar and serve at once, with cream if liked.

☐ *A good, quick last-minute pudding.*

For 4

Banana Soufflé

4 bananas
2 whole eggs, plus 2 whites
dash of rum
1 oz butter
1½ oz flour
½ pint milk
2 oz vanilla sugar

Butter a two-pint soufflé dish. Put three of the bananas in their skins into a moderate oven, Reg 4/350°, for about ten minutes, while you make a sauce with the butter, flour, milk and sugar. Remove the bananas and turn up the oven to Reg 7/425°.

While the sauce cools prepare the bananas by removing the skins, which have gone black, and pulping the fruit. Stir them into the sauce, and add the egg yolks and the rum, stirring all the time. Cut the remaining banana into cubes and stir it in.

Beat the egg whites to a firm snow and fold them into the sauce. Turn the mixture into the buttered soufflé dish, put it in the oven, turn down the heat to Reg 6/400° and cook for half an hour. Serve at once dusted with fine sugar.

For 4

Batter Pudding

Batter (page 60)
2 tablespoons butter, lard or oil
4 oz raisins, sultanas or currants, or all three mixed
golden syrup and cream

Make the batter two hours before you need it.
Preheat the oven to Reg 9/475°. Put two tablespoons
of fat in a baking tin and heat in the oven for a few
minutes. Stir the washed, thoroughly drained and
dried fruit into the batter, pour it into the very hot
fat and return it to the oven. After five minutes
lower the heat to Reg 6/400°, and cook 35–40
minutes.

Serve hot with warmed treacle and top of the milk
or cream.

For 4–6

Bread and Butter Pudding

6 slices assorted bread and butter (white, brown or
    currant loaf, or a mixture of all three)
handful of currants, raisins or sultanas
2 eggs
1 tablespoon sugar (preferably vanilla)
¾–1 pint milk

Lay the bread, crusts cut off, in a buttered pie dish
in layers, with fruit in between. Beat the eggs with
the sugar and add the milk. Pour over the bread and
leave to soak for half an hour or so. Cook in a low
oven, Reg 1/275°, for one hour, loosely covered with
greaseproof paper and for a further half hour,
uncovered, to puff and brown.

Serve with cream and more sugar.

For 4

Compôte of Fruit

1 lb washed fresh fruit
½ pint water
4 oz sugar

Heat the sugar and water in a saucepan and when the sugar has dissolved bring it to the boil and carefully put in the fruit. It will not be covered by the liquid so turn it over gently once or twice to coat it. Return to the boil and then turn the heat down as low as it will go, and cover the pan. Leave for ten minutes for soft fruit, 15 minutes or more for apples and pears; the fruit should be tender but still whole. Remove it carefully with a perforated spoon and put it in a glass or china bowl. Return the liquid to the heat and boil, uncovered, to a thickish syrup. Allow to cool, then pour it over the fruit.

☐ *Use plums, greengages, apricots, Morello cherries, peeled pears or apples, quartered or sliced.*

For 4

Clafoutis

2 eggs
3 oz sugar
1½ oz flour
¼ pint double cream
½ pint milk
1 lb stoned black cherries
kirsch (optional)

Preheat oven to Reg 5/375°. Cream the eggs and sugar in a basin, beating hard with an electric beater or wire whisk. Add the flour all at once, beat it in and add the cream, then the milk. Put the cherries in a shallow earthenware oven dish, pour over the batter and cook in the oven for 35 minutes. The batter should be brown on top and halfway between custard and cake inside. Eat it hot or cold with cream.

This is really delicious but can be improved slightly by the addition of a tiny glass of Kirsch just before the cream. The whole thing is rather indigestible but worth it.

☐ *You can use other fruit such as plums, apples and apricots, which are cheaper and more often available.*

For 4–6

Egg Custard

1 large egg
2 tablespoons vanilla sugar
½ pint milk

Julia's Rice Pudding

2 level tablespoons pudding rice
1 level tablespoon vanilla sugar, or plain sugar and
    vanilla essence
pinch salt
few chips lemon peel
1 teaspoon butter
1 pint milk

Mix the egg and sugar in a basin. Heat the milk to scalding point (almost boiling but not quite), pour it on to the egg, whisking as you do so. Return the mixture to the milk pan and heat gradually, without boiling of course, over a low heat, stirring constantly with a wooden spoon. When it has thickened enough to coat the spoon, take it off the heat.

☐ *For steamed and other puddings.*

Put the oven on the lowest possible heat. Take a saucepan and put in the milk, sugar, salt and lemon peel. Bring to the boil while you butter a one-pint pudding dish or pie dish. Turn the boiling milk and rice into the dish and leave it, uncovered, in your low, low oven for five hours. Remove the black skin before eating a really good, creamy, succulent dish of mother's favourite pudding. Eat it with cream and sugar.

☐ *For those who enjoy the skin keep the pudding covered for the first four hours, then allow to brown.*

For 4–5

Blackberry Water Ice

1 lb raw blackberries
4 oz sugar
¼ pint water
1 small egg white

Turn the refrigerator to its coldest setting. Make a syrup by boiling the sugar and water for four minutes. Allow it to cool. Sieve or mouli the blackberries and mix with the syrup. Beat the egg white until it forms soft peaks and fold thoroughly into the blackberry mixture. Put into a dish, cover and freeze to a mush. Stir and freeze for a further half hour. Stir again and freeze until set, about 2½–3 hours altogether.

☐ *This can also be made with raspberries or loganberries.*

For 4

Coffee Granita

4 oz vanilla sugar (page 188)
¾ pint hot, double strength coffee

Dissolve the sugar in the coffee, pour the mixture into the ice-making tray and freeze until mushy. Remove it to a bowl and beat with a fork. Return and freeze to sorbet consistency. Serve in glasses with a dollop of cream if you like.

For 4

Lemon Ice

8 oz sugar
juice of 2 lemons and grated rind of one
1½ pint milk
2 teaspoons gelatine crystals melted in 2 tablespoons
    water

Dissolve the sugar in the lemon juice. Add the milk and gelatine, stirring well. Add the finely grated rind of one lemon and freeze, covered, in the ice compartment of your refrigerator, turned to its coldest setting, for three hours. Stir the mixture twice during the setting time.

For 6

Grapefruit Sherbet

12 oz caster sugar
2 large grapefruit
¾ pint water
squeeze lemon juice
2 egg whites
tiny pinch salt

Stir the sugar and the finely grated rind of one of the grapefruit into the water in a thick saucepan. Heat gradually, stirring; when the sugar has dissolved, bring the mixture to the boil and boil fast for five minutes. Allow to cool, stir in the juice of the two grapefruits and a squeeze of lemon juice, and put in the freezer tray in the refrigerator; freeze to a mush.

Beat the egg whites to soft peaks with a little pinch of salt; fold them into the mush and freeze at the coldest setting on the refrigerator for half an hour. Whip until the egg whites are spread evenly through the mixture and freeze again for 2½–3 hours.

For 8

Caramelised Oranges

4 oranges
4 oz caster sugar
water

Peel the oranges over a plate with a very sharp knife, removing the peel and pithy skin at the same time. Slice carefully on the plate into thin slices, cut these in half, removing the pips and centre core.

Lay them on a dish like the scales of a fish. Caramelise the sugar with the orange juice collected on the plate and a couple of tablespoons of water. When the sugar turns golden brown watch it carefully darken to deep chestnut, then pour it in a thin layer over the sliced oranges.

Don't make this too far ahead of time because the caramel will lose its crispness.

For 4

Candied Oranges

6 large juicy seedless oranges
½ pint water
6 oz granulated sugar
liqueur (optional)

Use a very sharp stainless steel knife with a saw-edge to score each orange with long narrow cuts forming strips running from top to bottom of the fruit. Then peel these off with your knife, or a sharp potato peeler, as thinly as you can so that you have a heap of little pithless orange-peel matchsticks.

If you like a bland rather than a slightly bitter flavour, blanch the strips for one minute in boiling water and drain them well. Melt the sugar in the water and bring to the boil; poach the orange-peel strips in this syrup, uncovered, until tender, about 15 minutes. Put the oranges, stripped of every shred of pith and skin, on a dish, and pour the syrup over them; allow to cool. Arrange the shreds of peel in little mounds on top of each one. Every Italian restaurant seems to have these on the sweet trolley and they are always refreshing and delicious. You can add a liqueur such as Grand Marnier to the syrup if you want.

For 6

Orange Fritters

Fritter batter (page 60)
2 large oranges, seedless if possible
deep oil for frying
caster sugar

Peel the oranges very carefully, removing all the
white pith, but don't cut into the orange at all.
Break into pieces of two or three segments. Dip
each piece into the batter and fry in hot oil until
golden brown. Serve sprinkled with more sugar.

For 4

Orange Jellies

6 large oranges
1 packet orange jelly (to make 1 pint)

Cut the oranges across in halves and squeeze the
juice into a jug. Strain and measure it and use it,
made up with enough water, to make the orange
jelly. Remove all the skin and pith from inside the
orange halves so that each one makes a clean bowl,
and pour in the hot, dissolved jelly. Leave to set,
and when quite firm you can cut each half in two,
so they look like orange slices miraculously made of
jelly.

☐ *This is pure children's party food.*

For 6–12 children, depending on their size

Sweet Pancakes

½ lb plain flour
¾ pint milk and water, half and half
1 large or 2 small eggs
1 tablespoon melted butter or oil
1 tablespoon sugar
¼ teaspoon salt

Make the pancake batter at least two hours, and preferably more, before using it, as the starch granules need time to expand and absorb the liquid to make a really good pancake.

Put the sifted flour in a large mixing bowl, make a well in the centre and gradually add the milk and water, working the flour in with a wooden spoon. When all the flour is smoothly incorporated into the liquid, add the beaten eggs, melted butter or oil, sugar and salt, and beat the mixture thoroughly. It should have the consistency of thin cream. Add more milk if necessary, and then let it stand.

Have ready:
a frying pan
4 oz lard, cut into cubes the size of a sugar lump
a coffee cup
a large pan of hot water covered with a plate
a dozen strips of greaseproof paper, 1 inch wide,
and 3 inches longer than the diameter of the pan

The painstaking preparations make the cooking of the pancakes much faster and easier, so do not despair.

Heat the frying pan on a brisk heat, drop a lump of lard into it, and tip the pan from side to side so that the base is coated. Stir the batter and fill the coffee cup. Tilt the pan and pour the batter in at the highest point, rotating the pan to cover the base completely with a very thin layer of batter. It should set at once. Let it cook until it shifts when you shake the pan, then flip it over with a spatula, first making sure it is not sticking anywhere. Cook the other side, and slip the pancake on to the plate over the pan of hot water. Put a strip of paper across and continue cooking the pancakes and piling them up, with strips of paper in between, to prevent them from sticking together.

The pancakes are now ready to be filled or sprinkled with lemon and sugar. Experts flip the pancakes into the air to turn them and keep two pans going at once.

For 12–14 average pancakes

Orange Pancakes

8 thin pancakes, freshly made (opposite)
2 oranges
2 oz granulated sugar
4 oz butter

Grate oranges finely all over and mix the peel with the sugar. Soften the butter and beat the sugar into it, gradually adding the juice of the oranges. This butter can then be wrapped and chilled in the refrigerator until you need it; it keeps several days.

Put the orange butter in a frying pan over a moderate heat. When it starts to bubble lay a pancake in the pan, spoon the butter over it and then fold in it half and half again with a palette knife. Put the folded, juicy pancake on a hot dish, and put another one into the slowly bubbling sauce. Repeat the spooning and folding process until all the pancakes are used up; pour any extra butter over the folded parcels of pancake and serve immediately. You can also make this with lemons, using more sugar.

For 4

Sweet Pancakes with Cream Cheese

12 freshly made very thin pancakes (opposite)
8 oz cream cheese
1 egg yolk
2 oz caster sugar
2 oz raisins
2 oz chopped blanched almonds
1–2 oz butter

Put the cream cheese, beaten egg yolk and sugar in a bowl and beat together with a fork. Add the raisins and nuts and stir them in. Put a large dollop of the mixture in a strip in the middle of each pancake, and fold it over as if you were wrapping a parcel.

Heat the butter in the frying pan, drop in the little parcels, brown them all over and serve hot, sprinkled with caster sugar. You can serve cream with these.

☐ *These are very filling*.

For 6

Frosted Redcurrants 1

1 lb redcurrants on their stems
4 oz granulated sugar
½ pint water
caster sugar

Ricotta with Coffee

4 oz Ricotta (or cottage cheese)
2 tablespoons freshly ground coffee
1 teaspoon caster sugar
Cream (optional)

Carefully pick over and wash the currants if you are not sure they are clean. Shake off all the water. Make a syrup by boiling the granulated sugar with water for five minutes. Keeping the syrup gently on the boil, dip the branches of redcurrants first into the syrup, shaking off the extra drips, then into the caster sugar, shaking again. Then put them on a large flat dish covered with a white paper doily. It is easy if the currants are held by the end of the stalk or hooked on to the prongs of a fork, but they must only be dipped into the syrup for a moment and flicked in and out of the caster sugar. Lay them out side by side and let them harden as they dry — drying in the sun is ideal. They can be kept in the refrigerator until they are needed. Children adore them and they make a lovely end to a summer dinner party. It is rather fiddly and takes a long time but is still rather fun to do.

Sprinkle each person's helping of cheese with the sugar and ground coffee. That's all. Serve with cream if you have some.

For 2

Frosted Redcurrants 2

These are made as before but dipped into whipped egg whites instead of hot syrup. Turn them over from time to time as they dry. This is good if the currants are very ripe, but shop ones tend to be on the unripe side and less sweet as a result.

☐ *Serve ice-cold. Lovely to make on a fine summer's day.*

For 6

Strawberry Fool

½ pint double cream, as cold as possible
1 lb second-rate strawberries
6 oz caster sugar

Whisk the cream until it is softly thick, and gradually add five ounces of caster sugar. Whisk on until the cream stands in peaks, but is still soft; over-beating leaves you with a bowl full of butter.

Hull the strawberries, leaving a few of the best ones for decoration afterwards. Mash them to a pulp, the potato masher does this quickly, and add an ounce of caster sugar.

Fold the purée into the cream so that it is not really well mixed, and tip the whole thing into a pretty bowl or glass dish. Put the strawberries you kept for best on top and chill in the refrigerator.

☐ *This can be made just as well with raspberries. It is one of the great luxuries of high summer, both delicate and rich, and of a beautiful soft pink. It sounds extravagant but a little of it goes a long way, far further than plain strawberries and cream, and it makes use of fruit that may be past its best, which you could not eat whole.*

For 5–6

Summer Pudding

1 lb raspberries
½ lb redcurrants
½ lb blackcurrants
6–8 oz caster sugar
several slices white bread

Cook each kind of fruit separately with a few table-spoons of sugar and one tablespoon of water, to stop them catching on the pan before the juice starts to run out. They should be cooked as briefly as possible, the raspberries scarcely at all. Line a seven-inch pudding basin with medium slices of white bread, crusts removed, cutting them into wedge shapes to fit the sides of the bowl. Put in the redcurrants first, then the blackcurrants for the second layer and finally the raspberries, using all the fruit juice. On top put a layer of slices of bread (crusts removed as before), and cover with a saucer, slightly smaller in diameter than the pudding bowl. On this stand weights, which could be put inside a polythene bag in case the juice comes up over the top of the saucer. Leave overnight in the refrigerator and turn out carefully the following day.

☐ *This should be made the day before you want it.*

For 4–6

Roly Poly Pudding

½ lb flour, self-raising, or plain with 3 teaspoons
　　baking powder
5 oz shredded suet
pinch salt
2 tablespoons sugar
water
1 pot of jam
1 large doubled square of butter muslin, or a thick
　　clean tea-towel, scalded and thickly floured
6 pins

Put a large pan of water on to boil. Make a suet
pastry by mixing the flour, suet, salt and sugar with
a knife and adding enough water to make a stiff
dough. Roll it out on the floured cloth so that it
forms a rectangle about 9 × 18 inches. Spread jam or
treacle thickly down the middle, leaving a margin of
about two inches at the sides and at one end. Brush
the margin with cold water, then roll up the pastry
lightly, as if making a Swiss roll, starting at the
jammy end. Squeeze the ends together firmly and
pat the join to seal it.

Roll the cloth loosely round the pudding, allowing
for it to swell in cooking. Pin the side and ends, and
fold the ends to form a handle. Drop the pudding
into boiling water (it should float) and boil, covered,
for two hours. Add more boiling water from time to
time. Carefully remove the cloth and all the pins,
and serve with hot jam.

Instead of spreading the pastry with jam you can
cover it with a layer of currants and raisins (Spotted
Dick), or stoned chopped dates, or with chopped
rhubarb or apple, or stoned plums.

For 6

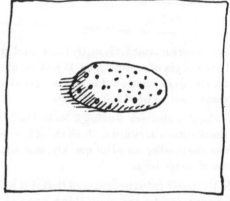

1 Lay pudding in scalded, floured cloth

2 Wrap and pin it as shown

**3 Bend over and pin the ends to
form a handle**

Treacle Sponge

for top of pudding
2–3 tablespoons golden syrup
juice of ½ lemon
½ teaspoon caraway seeds
small handful breadcrumbs

4 oz butter, 4 oz sugar
2 eggs, beaten
teaspoon grated lemon rind
5 oz self-raising flour
pinch of salt, milk to mix

Mix the syrup, lemon juice, caraway seeds and breadcrumbs in the bottom of a buttered two-pint pudding basin. Cream the butter and sugar together until fluffy, add the beaten eggs and the lemon rind and then the flour with a pinch of salt. Add a little milk to bring the mixture to a dropping consistency. Turn it into the basin, on top of the treacle and lemon juice mixture, cover well with a double layer of greased greaseproof paper and a cloth, or double aluminium foil, and steam for two hours, covered, in a large pan of water.

Serve, turned out, with more golden syrup, warmed, and cream if there is some available.

For 6

Six-Cup Pudding

Use an ordinary teacup that contains half a pint.
1 cup sugar
1 cup butter (7 oz)
1 beaten egg
1 cup raisins
1 cup currants
1 cup self-raising flour, or 1 cup plain flour and ½
    teaspoon baking powder
1 teaspoon mixed spice
1 cup milk

Cream the sugar and butter together, add the egg, fruit, and then the flour, baking powder and spice. Moisten with milk, beating the mixture until it drops off the spoon. You may not need all the milk. Turn it into a greased basin, cover and steam for 2½ hours.

☐ *Serve this with home-made custard (page 195) for a very good, thoroughly British, rib-sticking pudding.*

For 6–8

Treacle Tart

for pastry:
6 oz self-raising flour
3 oz cooking fat
pinch salt
water to mix
4 oz fresh brown breadcrumbs
1 cup golden syrup

Toffee Sauce

1 oz butter
3 oz brown sugar
2 tablespoons golden syrup
4 tablespoons cream

Make the pastry and let it stand in a cool place for at least half an hour. Preheat the oven to Reg 6/400°. Grease an eight-inch flan tin and line it with the pastry. Fill with breadcrumbs and pour the syrup over generously. Use the pastry trimmings to make a slender lattice over the syrup. Bake for 20–30 minutes and eat hot.

For 4–6

Put all the ingredients in a small saucepan and heat together gently until hot and melted, but not boiling. Serve hot.

☐ *For vanilla ice cream.*

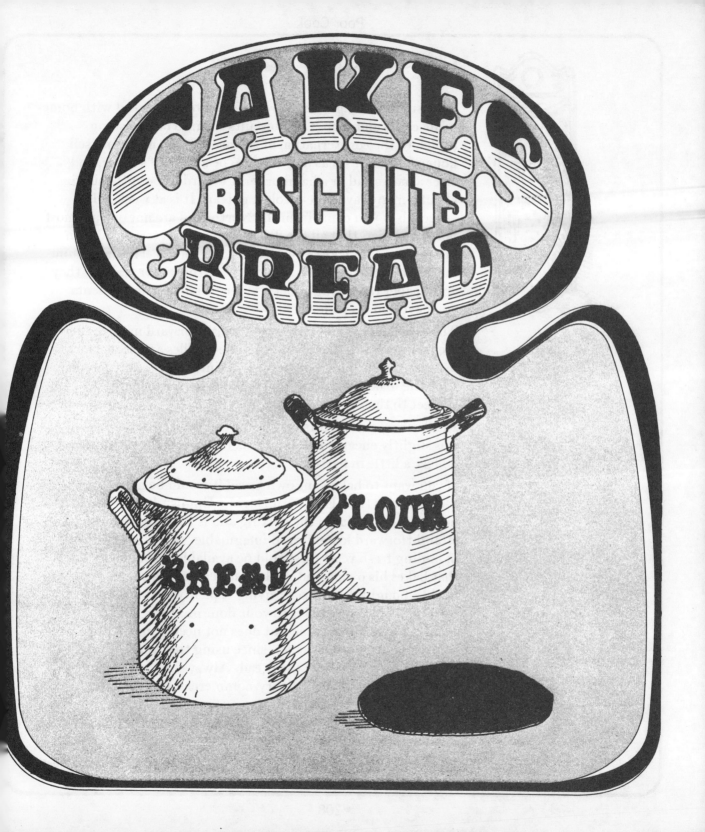

CAKES BISCUITS & BREAD

Cakes, Biscuits and Bread

Like suet puddings, huge great teas at tables spread with home-made cakes and scones and biscuits seem to be vanishing (much to the consternation of the people who make and sell flour). Children's teas now seem to be a form of supper, and after a ham salad or a hamburger it is hard to be enthusiastic about a many-layered chocolate gâteau. It is at weekends, especially if you come from the North, and are not on an almost perpetual diet, that all the delicious buns and tea-breads can be tried, and it makes a very cosy sight. You feel like a genuine mother or wife if there are home-made things for tea, and they are cheaper than bought ones, and contain only ingredients you have chosen yourself.

These recipes are all of a simple straightforward nature; there are no flights into the realms of mille-feuilles and sachertorte because the authors have never had time to get really familiar with the making of them, and feel it is better to leave the subject to those who love cake-making.

In all cakes and biscuits margarine can be used instead of butter; it is slightly cheaper and it creams faster, but the end products do lose a little in flavour.

If you want to bake your own bread it would be hard to find a recipe better than Elizabeth David's English Loaf,* which uses no sugar and no fat in the making and is the most delicious straightforward loaf of bread imaginable. If you have difficulty in finding fresh yeast (it should be available through any baker that bakes his own bread, and most health food shops) try using freshly-bought dried yeast, giving it plenty of time to get working before you add it to your flour mixture. It likes a few grains of sugar to feed on, but does not need as much as is recommended on the packet, since using that amount might spoil the plain nature of the bread. Always buy special bread flour to make a loaf; ordinary commercial flour is finely milled specially for the making of pastry, cakes and so on, and is not good for bread. If you can find unbleached white flour it makes a loaf with a very good flavour.

* Elizabeth David *The Baking of an English Loaf*, available from Elizabeth David Ltd., 46 Bourne Street, London, S.W.1.

Plain Sponge Cake

4 oz caster sugar
4 oz unsalted butter
4 oz self-raising flour, or 4 oz plain flour plus 1 ½
   teaspoons baking powder
2 eggs

Preheat the oven to Reg 5/375°. Butter and flour two eight-inch sandwich tins. Cream the sugar and butter together and when white and fluffy add the well-beaten eggs, a little at a time. Fold in the sifted flour thoroughly.

Spread half the mixture in each tin as lightly as you can, spreading it to the sides with a palette knife so that the finished cake will be flat rather than domed.

Bake in the top half of the oven for 15–20 minutes. Do not open the oven while the cakes are cooking or they may go sad. When they are cooked take them out and cool on a wire rack. Spread one half with whipped cream and the other with jam. Press the halves together so jam and cream are both in the middle.

Quick Sponge Cake

4 oz soft margarine
4 oz caster sugar
2 eggs
4 oz self-raising flour
1 level teaspoon baking powder

Preheat the oven to Reg 5/375°. Butter and flour two seven-inch Victoria sponge tins.

Sieve everything into a bowl and beat at top speed for 40 seconds. Turn the mixture into the prepared tins, flatten the top with a palette knife and bake for 15–20 minutes. Fill the middle with raspberry jam and cream, and sprinkle the top with sugar.

If the mixture is ready before the oven is up to full heat, put it in the refrigerator to check the action of the raising agent.

☐ *This mixture takes about 40 seconds to make with an electric beater. Don't be tempted to give it longer as overbeating toughens the cake. The trick is to use one of the specially soft margarines, which won't go solid even in the refrigerator.*
The sponge is made and cooked in less than half an hour.

Madeleines

2 eggs and their weight in :
caster sugar (vanilla sugar if possible)
unsalted butter, softened
self-raising flour

juice of ½ lemon

Preheat the oven to Reg 5/375°. Separate the egg yolks from the whites. Beat the yolks and sugar together in a basin until white and fluffy. Add the butter softened to a creamy consistency, and beat away until the mixture is smooth. Beat in the flour and lemon juice and finally the egg whites, broken up with a fork but not beaten. Butter the madeleine tins which have shell-shaped indentations, or shallow jam tart tins and put a spoonful of the mixture, about the size of a walnut, in each well. Bake in the centre of the oven for 15–20 minutes. Beware — they can go from not cooked to burned in a very short time. They should be brown round the edges. Eat them the same day if you can ; they are very crisp outside, light and soft inside.

Makes 24–30

Carolina Biscuits

½ lb margarine
6 oz pale soft brown sugar
1 egg white
1–2 teaspoons cinnamon
1 teaspoon ground ginger
pinch salt
10 oz flour

Preheat the oven to Reg 5/375° and grease two baking sheets. Beat the margarine with the sugar, egg white, spices and pinch of salt, using a wire whisk or electric beater. When it is thoroughly creamed add the flour and beat it in. Spread the mixture thinly on baking sheets with a spatula and bake 10–15 minutes to a nice golden brown. The mixture may seem very wet before cooking ; spread it on the tins with well-floured hands if this is easier.

Cut the mixture in diamond shapes while it is hot. These biscuits should be thin, fragile and spicy.

Makes about 48

Plain Biscuit Mixture

4 oz unsalted butter
4 oz caster sugar
8 oz plain flour
1 small egg

Scotch Cookies

1 egg
4 oz caster sugar
2 oz butter, softened
¼ pint milk
1 lb self-raising flour, or less

Cream the sugar and butter together, add the beaten egg, stir in the sifted flour, mix to a firm dough. Ideally leave it to rest in the refrigerator, but if in a hurry carry on. Set the oven to Reg 5/375°. Roll the dough thinly and cut into shapes. At places like Fortnum & Mason they cut them into stars and moons, oakleaves and acorns. Place the shapes in a buttered and floured tin, brushing some with beaten egg, if liked. Put the tin near the top of the oven for ten minutes or until done. Leave to cool and crisp on the tin and then on a wire rack.

Variations: dip half of each biscuit (especially for acorns and oakleaves) into melted chocolate; or cover with white icing, flavoured with vanilla or almond essence.

You can add ginger or vanilla or chopped nuts to the mixture before baking.

☐ *This is so easy that children can make it by themselves.*

Preheat the oven to Reg 7½/435°. Cream the egg and sugar together, add the softened butter, beat it in, mix in the milk and then add enough flour to make the mixture the consistency of pastry. Roll out to quarter-inch thickness on a floured board, cut into two-inch circles with a glass or pastry-cutter and place on a buttered and floured baking-sheet. Bake just above the middle of the oven for 12 minutes; they will rise and go golden brown. Serve warm, sliced in half with butter and jam and cream. Next day they can be halved and toasted. Don't let anybody think that you were really trying to make scones.

☐ *This is a sort of hybrid, halfway between a biscuit and a scone.*

Makes 24

Derby Sage Cheese Straws

6 oz plain flour
salt, pepper, and a pinch cayenne
4 oz butter
1 egg yolk
4 oz finely grated Derby Sage cheese
1 tablespoon water

Preheat the oven to Reg 5/375°. Sift the flour with the seasoning into a mixing bowl, drop in the butter and cut it into the flour. Rub it in lightly and quickly with your fingertips until the mixture looks like breadcrumbs, Add the cheese and stir it in with a knife. Mix the egg yolk and water, add to the dry ingredients and mix quickly to a firm dough. Knead lightly until smooth and chill for half an hour before rolling it out to about $\frac{1}{4}$ inch thick. Cut into narrow strips about two inches long. Bake on a lightly greased baking sheet until cooked, 15–20 minutes; they will be a lovely freckled greeny colour.

□ *This recipe is perfectly suitable for Cheddar or Cheshire cheese.*

Five-minute Ballater Scones

8 oz flour, 1 level teaspoon cream of tartar and $\frac{1}{2}$ small teaspoon bicarbonate of soda, or use 8 oz self-raising flour plus a pinch of baking powder
1 $\frac{1}{2}$ oz butter
$\frac{1}{4}$ teaspoon salt
scant $\frac{1}{4}$ pint tepid milk (sour is good)

Preheat the oven to Reg 7$\frac{1}{2}$/435°. Sieve the flour, cream of tartar, bicarbonate of soda and salt into a bowl. Rub in the butter at top speed, stir in enough milk to make a slightly stiff dough, and knead the mixture lightly in the bowl. Roll out to half-inch thickness on a floured board and cut into two-inch rounds. Put them on a buttered baking sheet and place them just above the centre of the oven. When they are nicely puffed up and pale golden, after 10 to 15 minutes, take them out and brush the tops with milk. Eat them warm.

Makes 12 scones

Dropscones

8 oz self-raising flour
½ teaspoon salt
1 oz caster sugar
1 beaten egg
just over ¼ pint milk, preferably sour, or buttermilk
lard to grease the griddle

Heat the griddle. Mix the dry ingredients in a bowl; make a well in the centre and add the egg and half the milk. Stir until the mixture is thick and smooth, then add the rest of the milk gradually, stirring all the time, until it is the consistency of cream. Pour into a jug.

Rub a piece of lard the size of a hazelnut quickly over the hot griddle on the point of a knife. Pour the batter on to the griddle in rounds about two inches across. Fry them till bubbles appear on the surface and the undersides are light brown. Flip them over with a palette knife and brown the other sides. Add more lard to the griddle and start again. As each batch is finished put it into a folded tea-towel to keep soft and warm.

Serve hot with plenty of butter.

Makes 15–20 scones

Midlothian Oatcakes

8 oz oatmeal (fine or coarse — porridge oats will do)
4 oz flour
½ teaspoon or more salt
1 teaspoon baking powder
water
3 oz butter, or half butter and half lard

Place the oatmeal in a basin. Sift in the flour, salt and baking powder. Rub in the fat and mix to a stiff dough with cold water. Turn the dough on to a board sprinkled with oatmeal, knead lightly and roll out to ⅛ inch thickness. Cut into rounds with a glass or teacup and bake in a moderate oven, Reg 4/350°, for 25 minutes. They should not brown, or only very slightly. Eat with butter for tea; they are also very good with cheese, at the end of a meal.

Makes about 20

Moyna's Irish Bread

9 heaped tablespoons wholewheat flour (½ lb)
2 heaped tablespoons plain flour
1 level teaspoon brown sugar
1 heaped teaspoon salt
1 heaped teaspoon baking powder
½ pint sour milk or buttermilk

Preheat the oven to Reg 8½/460°. Mix the dry ingredients in a bowl; add enough sour milk to make a soft dough. It may take less than half a pint. Turn the mixture into a buttered and floured bread tin and bake 35–40 minutes. When it is cooked wrap it in a clean, damp tea-cloth and put it on a wire rack to cool. This prevents the crust from becoming too crumbly.

If you have not got any sour milk, add a little lemon juice to some fresh milk and stir it well.

□ *This loaf should be crumbly and quite light. It is mixed in a couple of minutes and is a very good bread for tea.*

Cinnamon Toast

1 teaspoon ground cinnamon
3 teaspoons caster sugar
2 pieces hot buttered toast

Mix the sugar and cinnamon together and sprinkle on to the toast; eat straight away, hot and melting and spicy. Lovely for a winter tea.

For 2

Mrs Fitch's Walnut Bread

1 lb self-raising flour
1 level teaspoon salt
1 oz lard
4 oz walnut pieces
4 oz dates
3 oz sugar
1 egg
½ pint milk

Preheat oven to Reg 4½/360°. Sieve the flour and salt and rub in the lard. Chop the walnuts and dates and mix them into the rubbed flour together with the sugar. Beat the egg in the milk and mix it into the dry ingredients thoroughly, making a soft dough. You may not need all the liquid. Turn into a well-greased bread tin and bake in the oven for about an hour. Allow to cool and butter the slices like ordinary bread. Very good for tea.

Walnut Open Sandwiches

Spread good fresh white or wholemeal bread with butter and cover with fresh (if possible) walnut halves. Sprinkle with a little coarse salt and eat. A few walnuts will go a very long way and they make a delicious elevenses.

Miscellaneous

Crabapple Jelly

crabapples
water
sugar
bowl
tea-towel
string
jam jars
covers

You can flavour this with cloves, ginger or cinnamon. Pick out any unsound or bruised crabapples, and wash the rest well. Leave the stalks on, put in a saucepan and just cover with water. Simmer covered until they are a pulpy mass (about 30 minutes) prodding with a wooden spoon occasionally. Add the cloves, ginger or cinnamon now, if wanted. Wet a clean tea-towel or similar cloth, in hot water and wring it out. Put it over a basin large enough to hold all the apple juice, pour the pulpy apples and juice into it, tie it tightly with string and hang it over the bowl on a convenient hook or nail. (Use the cup hooks on the dresser.) Let it drip about 12 hours.

Measure the liquid (it will be cloudy but never mind, it clears with the sugar), put it in a large pan and add 1 lb sugar per pint of juice. Stir over gentle heat until the sugar is melted. Then bring to a fierce boil, so it froths up high, which is why you need a large pan. Stir all the time, skimming, and test for jelling, by putting a little to cool on a saucer

(when it wrinkles as you push it, it is ready) or when the drips are slow to leave the spoon if you hold it up over the pan. If you overboil, it will burn or go syrupy. If you underboil, it will be too runny and ferment. One pint can be ready in as little as ten minutes. Pour into clean hot jam jars, which should be waiting in the oven. Cover when cold.

Very good eaten with sugared petit suisse.

Seville Orange Marmalade

10 good Seville oranges
2 lemons
10 lbs sugar (preserving sugar is best because it dissolves well, but granulated will do)
9 pints water
a muslin bag to cook the pips in

To make a year's supply for an average small family you need four times this amount, but 15 lbs is a convenient quantity to cook, providing you have a large preserving pan.

The oranges are only here for a short time in January but it really is worth making your own marmalade; it costs half as much as shop marmalade and is twice as good. This method is spread over three days, but doesn't take much time on the second and third days.

1st day: halve and squeeze the juice from the ten oranges and two lemons. Sieve the juice to retain the pips. Shred the squeezed skins into large or small matchsticks, whichever you prefer, or if you are not fussy put them through the coarsest blade of your mincer. Pour eight pints of cold water over the peel and juice, and in a separate basin one pint of cold water over the pips. Leave to soak for 24 hours.

2nd day: strain the pips and put them in the muslin bag. Add their liquid to the peel and, in a preserving pan, simmer the pips with the peel very gently until the peel is quite tender. (Test by biting or by squeezing between finger and thumb). Do this in a pan with a lid; it takes about 1½ hours, but doesn't need watching or stirring. When tender leave the whole thing to soak another 24 hours.

3rd day: put fifteen clean 1 lb jam jars to heat in a low oven. Remove the bag of pips, pressing it to squeeze out all the juice which is an important source of pectin. Bring the marmalade to the boil in a large pan. Add the sugar, stirring well or it will burn. Boil very fast after the sugar has dissolved until setting point is reached, in 30–40 minutes. Test for setting by letting a little marmalade cool on a saucer or by holding up your spoon and waiting for the drips to become large, slow and heavy. Towards the end, take the pan off the heat while you wait for the results of the testing. Overcooking will produce a syrup that never sets, and under-cooking produces a sloppy mess that won't keep, but this marmalade sets beautifully and keeps two or three years. When it is absolutely ready, turn off the heat and allow to cool a little; it will soon start setting in the pan, so have your jars ready. Fill the jars, which should be standing on a board or newspapers, wipe them clean, allow them to cool and cover them carefully.

Makes 15 lbs

Fruit Syrups

1 lb preserving sugar to 1 pint juice
water

Put the fruit in a large china or earthenware basin with about ½ pint water to 3 lbs fruit and mash it down a bit with a wooden spoon or steak-beater. Stand the bowl, covered with a large lid, in a pan of water and put it in a slowish oven Reg 1/275° for one to two hours, mashing from time to time.

When the fruit seems to have softened as much as possible, take it out of the oven and strain it through a double muslin or jelly-bag, overnight if possible.

Next day add ¾–1 lb preserving sugar to each pint of juice, depending on how sweet you want the syrup. Add a little bag of cloves or cinnamon, or a dash of brandy or lemon juice if you like. Heat gently, stirring, in a large pan until the sugar is dissolved — no longer, or it will set like jam. Cool.

Have ready some small sterilised bottles, with sterilised screw caps (15 minutes in boiling water does the trick). Fill them with the syrup to within 1½–2 inches from the top and put on the screw tops. Without this space, the expanding hot liquid will burst the bottle when you sterilise it. Stand the bottles in a deep pan with a false bottom, a pressure cooker is ideal, and pour in water almost to the top of the bottles. Bring the water to the boil and keep boiling for 20–30 minutes. Take out the bottles and stand them on a wooden table or on folded news-papers, not on a cold surface or they will crack. When they have cooled tighten the screw tops if necessary and seal by dipping in melted wax, or with sticky tape.

Fruit syrup, as opposed to fruit squash, is incredibly expensive to buy and much nicer to drink. If there is a glut of any soft fruit such as blackberries, rasp-berries, blackcurrants, English grapes, strawberries, cherries etc., you can make your own. It will keep quite well until it is opened, after which it must be kept in the refrigerator.

It is very good in milk shakes or used as a sauce for a pudding, or of course as a base for a hot or cold drink.

Tomato Ketchup

6 lbs ripe tomatoes
½ lb onions
½ lb sugar
⅛ oz paprika
pinch cayenne
1½ oz salt
1 fluid oz wine vinegar (chilli or tarragon)
spiced vinegar:
½ pint wine vinegar
small piece cinnamon bark
10 whole allspice
6 cloves
2–3 blades of mace
1–2 bayleaves
1 chilli pepper

Make the spiced vinegar: put the spices into the wine vinegar, bring it to the boil, take it off the heat and leave for two hours, covered. Then strain.

Slice the tomatoes and peel the onions; cook them covered until the tomato skins start to come away. Rub the pulp through a sieve, add sugar, salt, cayenne and paprika. Cook until the sauce thickens, then add the spiced vinegar and wine vinegar. Cook until the sauce thickens again to the consistency of thick cream.

Pour into hot bottles with sterilised tops and seal firmly. Leave to mature a month or two.

☐ *One pound of tomatoes makes about half a pint of ketchup, so this is only worth doing if you have masses of tomatoes and ready appetites for ketchup.*

German Green Tomato Pickle

5 lbs green tomatoes, small enough to eat whole
2 pints cheap malt vinegar
1 lb white sugar
6 cloves, 1 inch cinnamon stick, and a piece of nutmeg or 2–3 blades mace (½ teaspoon powdered)
1 pint white wine vinegar
pinch salt

Remove the stalks from the tomatoes and put them, with their skins still on, in a large pan with the malt vinegar. Bring slowly to the boil, stirring. Then strain, put the tomatoes in a china bowl, and throw the vinegar away.

Bring the sugar, spices, wine vinegar and salt to the boil, stirring to dissolve the sugar, and pour it over the tomatoes. Leave in the bowl for 24 hours; next day, remove the tomatoes, boil up the liquid again, leave it to cool and pour it again over the tomatoes. Leave it for another 24 hours. The following day, bring the tomatoes and the liquid to the boil together, remove the tomatoes, and reduce the liquid until it becomes slightly syrupy. Remove the spices. Put the tomatoes into clean hot jars, pour over the syrup, slightly cooled, cover and keep at least three months.

☐ *This takes three days to make and is ready to eat in three months. It is very sweet and delicious and looks beautiful, quite unlike anything you can buy at the grocer.*

Making Flan cases

This is for savoury flans or sweet flans such as apple that don't need a very rich, short, sweet pastry. Have some dried beans or spaghetti shells that you always use for flans. Keep them in a specific place and then the whole performance becomes miraculously easy. Throw them out every so often and start with fresh ones, as they develop a strong smell of burned flour which could transmit itself to the flan.

Method:
(1) Preheat the oven to Reg 5/375°.
(2) Butter a 7–8 inch flan tin with a loose bottom.
(3) Roll out the pastry (page 218) to ⅛″ to ¼″ thickness.
(4) Line the flan tin with pastry lifted into place on the rolling pin. Trim the edges with a generous hand as the pastry does shrink.
(5) Prick the bottom all over with a fork.
(6) Line the flan case with a round piece of greaseproof paper.
(7) Spill in the beans.
(8) Put it into the oven for 15 minutes.
(9) Take it out of the oven, remove the beans and paper.

(10) Cook it a further ten minutes until the bottom is no longer soggy. It is now ready to be filled with a quiche mixture, apples or whatever you like and cooked in the normal way.

Plain Pie or Flan Pastry

6 oz plain flour
1½ oz slightly salted butter
1½ oz cooking fat
½ teaspoon salt, cold water

Sieve the flour and salt into a bowl. Chop the butter and cooking fat into it with a knife and then rub it in, lifting your hands several inches above the bowl with each movement, so that the fat is cooled by the air as it falls into the bowl; this may sound far-fetched but it really helps keep the pastry cool and therefore light. When it looks like fine breadcrumbs, carefully add water as you mix the pastry with your other hand until you have a light firm dough. Knead it together lightly, to distribute the moisture evenly. Stand it in a cool place, wrapped or covered, for at least an hour, before rolling out.

Yorkshire Pudding

4 oz plain flour, salt
2 eggs, ½ pint milk
2–3 tablespoons oil or good dripping

Make the batter by sieving the flour and salt into a bowl, make a well in the centre and add the eggs, breaking the yolks with your spoon before you start stirring. Add the milk gradually, stirring in the flour little by little until half the milk is added; keep going until all the flour is taken up and the mixture is smooth. Then add the rest of the milk and beat for five or ten minutes. Stand the batter in a cool place for one hour. Preheat oven to Reg 9/475°. When the batter is ready, heat the oil or dripping in a baking tin, pour on the batter and cook five minutes at Reg 9/475° and 35–40 minutes at Reg 7/425°.

☐ *Batter to be made two hours in advance.*

For 6

Melba Toast

To eat with potted meat, pâté and of course caviar. It looks twice as expensive as ordinary toast and costs even less.

Make toast in the usual way with slices of bread about quarter of an inch thick. Cut off the crusts and slice each piece of toast carefully in half through the soft centre, making two slices from one, each toasted on one side only.

Turn the grill down to a moderate heat and toast the thin slices gently on their untoasted side. They will curl slightly, and should be served hot, in a crisp pile.

You can make this toast in advance and reheat in a low oven before serving.

To freshen a stale loaf

Useful for the end of a long Easter or Christmas holiday.

Hold the loaf (or part of a loaf) in the steam of a kettle for one or two minutes, then leave it in a hot oven, Reg 8/450°, for five minutes. When cool the crust will be as crisp as newly baked bread.

Home-made Breadcrumbs

Collect all the left-over ends of loaves, making sure that none are going mouldy. Put them in a very low oven, or all day in the plate-warming drawer of your cooker, until they are completely dried and pale brown.

Lay a tea-towel on a firm table. Fold it neatly round the bread so that the crumbs cannot escape, and press a rolling pin all over it, crushing and crunching the bread. Hold a sieve over a baking tin and shake the crumbs through. Repeat the performance until the crusts are all fine crumbs. Store them in an airtight jar, and they will keep well.

Babies' Rusks

Cut stale bread into fingers and dry in the oven. Babies will never guess they didn't come out of a packet.

Mr Hale's Method of Peeling Chestnuts

Put a tablespoon of vegetable oil in a roasting tin to warm in the oven. Score the chestnuts, cutting through to the inner skin, then place them in the tin and swirl around until they are coated in oil. Bake in the oven at Reg 5/375° for 15–20 minutes. The oil prevents burning and the skins are easy to remove.

Another Method

Score the chestnuts and boil 10–15 minutes. Remove the shells. Return to the pan and boil for 20–30 minutes when the skins will be easy to remove.

Coconut Ice

2 lbs sugar
just over ¼ pint milk
1 oz butter
8 oz desiccated coconut
pink colouring

Put the sugar, butter and milk in a heavy saucepan and bring them slowly to the boil, stirring to dissolve the sugar. Boil for four minutes stirring all the time. Remove from the heat, add the coconut, stir well and pour half into a greased tin, one inch deep. Colour the other half and pour into a separate tin. Mark into fingers when it is half set, and cut when cool. It sets quickly so you should work fast. It is very good for Christmas presents and bazaars.

Lemonade

5 lemons
1 ½ lbs granulated sugar
1 pint boiling water
½ oz citric acid

Thinly pare the lemons (no white) with a sharp knife or potato peeler, and pour one pint of boiling water on to this peel. Add the sugar and the juice of the lemons. Stir until the sugar dissolves, steep overnight and strain. Stir in the citric acid. Use diluted. This lemonade keeps for weeks in screw-top bottles in the refrigerator.

Makes 1½ pints concentrated juice

Muesli

This recipe was one of dozens sent by angry readers after an article in the Sunday Times saying bought muesli was better than home-made.

The night before, soak rolled oats in enough milk to cover, add sugar, chopped fresh apple (unpeeled), nuts, raisins, apricots, or any other fruit available. Stir thoroughly and leave overnight. Just before serving add cream, sliced banana and lemon juice.

Pretend Cream

1 peeled sliced banana
1 white of egg
2 teaspoons sugar

Beat the banana with the sugar and egg white until the banana totally vanishes. Use it as you would whipped cream for children's puddings, jellies, meringues and cakes.

This wouldn't really fool anybody but it's quite good if you are out of cream.

To Clarify Butter

Clarified butter keeps better than ordinary butter and is used to seal up pâtés and home-made potted game and meat. It is also excellent for frying; it is the milk content in butter that makes it burn, and this is filtered out in the clarifying. It is also the nearest thing to ghee for making Indian curries.

It is not worth clarifying less than half a pound because you lose quite a lot on the way; more is worthwhile, since it keeps so well. Use the cheapest butter.

Melt the butter slowly in a thick saucepan, without browning. Turn off the heat, stir it and let it stand for a few minutes to settle. Line a sieve with a fine cloth squeezed out in hot water and stand it over a bowl. Pour in the butter and let it drip through. Allow to set and remove it from the bowl; pour away the water from underneath.

Clarified butter should be a lovely, even, semi-transparent yellow colour.

To Clarify Fat

The sort of fat which is left from a pot-au-feu or other lengthy boiling of meat is not very suitable for immediate use, as it is full of moisture and fragments of meat and vegetables.

To clarify it, put it in a pan with double its quantity of water. Bring it all to the boil, allow it to cool and the fat will form a solid disc above the water, with some of the pieces and fragments stuck underneath (the rest should be in the water). Scrape all the pieces off and melt the fat down again; pour it into a pot.

It is worth doing this with pork, beef or chicken fat.

Yoghurt

1 heaped teaspoon plain yoghurt
1 quart fresh milk (the amount of milk used makes the same amount of yoghurt)

Bring the milk to the boil over a high flame. When it starts to rise in the pan take it off the heat and allow to cool until you can keep your finger in while you count ten (110°–120°). Put the starting teaspoon of yoghurt in a bowl and stir in the milk. Put the bowl in a warm place, wrapped in a folded towel, and leave it undisturbed for six to eight hours. Overnight is ideal. Unwrap the bowl. You should now have yoghurt with water on top; if not put it back for a while, otherwise pour off the water and chill the yoghurt.

The first batch is not always as good as it might be, because bought yoghurt has often been deep-frozen, but using your own yoghurt as a starter will make a good second batch — each subsequent batch will become increasingly weak.

☐ *Also known as Persian Milk, yoghurt is a very ancient food and is supposed to promote longevity.*

Beurre Manié

Mash together an equal amount of butter and flour and squeeze it in the palm of your hand to combine the two elements properly.

Use it to thicken stews and sauces at the end of the cooking.

Cure for Indigestion

Boiled water, drunk as hot as possible.

Index